PCs

by Shelley O'Hara

in 10 Minutes

SAMS

A Division of Macmillan Computer Publishing
201 West 103rd St., Indianapolis, Indiana 46290 USA

©1998 by Sams Corporation

International Standard Book Number: 0-672-31322-7
Library of Congress Catalog Card Number: 98-84599

99 98   8 7 6 5 4 3

Interpretation of the printing code: the rightmost number of the first series of numbers is the year of the book's printing; the rightmost number of the second series of numbers is the number of the book's printing. For example, a printing code of 98-1 shows that the first printing of the book occurred in 1998.

Screen reproductions in this book were created by means of the program Collage Plus from Inner Media, Inc., Hollis, NH.

Printed in the United States of America

Publisher John Pierce

Editorial Services Director Carla Hall

Managing Editor Thomas F. Hayes

Acquisitions Editor Angela Wethington

Production Editor Maureen A. McDaniel

Technical Editor Dave Shinn

Cover Designer Dan Armstrong

Production Trey Frank, Laura A. Knox, Tony McDonald, Paul Wilson

Indexer Tim Taylor

WE'D LIKE TO HEAR FROM YOU!

Sams Corporation has a long-standing reputation for high-quality books and products. To ensure your continued satisfaction, we also understand the importance of customer service and support.

TECH SUPPORT

If you need assistance with the information in this book, please access Macmillan Computer Publishing's online Knowledge Base at **http://www.superlibrary.com/general/support**. If you do not find the answer to your questions on our Web site, you may contact Macmillan Technical Support by phone at **317/581-3833** or via e-mail at **support@mcp.com**.

ORDERS, CATALOGS, AND CUSTOMER SERVICE

To order other Macmillan Computer Publishing books, catalogs, or products, please contact our Customer Service Department at **800/428-5331** or fax us at **800/835-3202** (International Fax: 317/228-4400). Or visit our online bookstore at **http://www.mcp.com/**.

TRADEMARKS

All terms mentioned in this book that are known to be trademarks have been appropriately capitalized. Sams cannot attest to the accuracy of this information. Use of a term in this book should not be regarded as affecting the validity of any trademark or service mark.

ABOUT THE AUTHOR

Shelley O'Hara has written over 25 computer books and is one of Sams best-selling authors. She is an independent technical writer and consultant in Indianapolis.

CONTENTS

Introduction to PCs

Have you recently bought a PC? Or are you thinking of purchasing a PC? Or maybe you've had a PC for some time, but still aren't sure what each piece and part does. If so, you might want a short little book to tell you all the basic stuff you need to know about using a computer. This is that book.

Why This Book?

This book is perfect for a computer user that just wants the basic facts about using a PC without a lot of technical jargon. Here's why:

- The book is broken down into 22 lessons, all easily read in ten minutes or less. You don't have to spend a lot of time wading through long chapters and complicated explanations.

- The book focuses on the key things you *have* to know so that you can get comfortable using a PC. You don't have to learn each and every little thing about a PC. By focusing on what you need to know, you can build your skills more easily.

- The book covers just about all the main topics of using a PC. You learn about hardware, software, and Windows 95. You learn the basic tasks for working with software as well as exploring the Internet. These are the things you will do day after day after day. You may not need to learn too much more than what is covered here.

- This book contains lots of step-by-step instructions for common tasks. You can use these steps to learn how to perform these key tasks on your PC. The step-by-step procedures are also illustrated with figures so that you know what you should see on your screen.

ICONS USED IN THE BOOK

In addition to the background information and step-by-step instructions, the book contains other useful tips, cautions, and definitions, each identified with an icon:

 Timesaver Tips   You can review these tips to find out shortcuts and other timesaving advice.

 Panic Button   Read these cautions to avoid common mistakes and potential problems.

 Plain English   Computer technology includes a lot of jargon. Look for these icons to define common terms.

Use this book on your journey to learning about computers. Good Luck!

WHAT IS A COMPUTER?

In this lesson, you learn a basic description of a computer including definitions of hardware and software.

DEFINING A PC

A personal computer (PC) is an electronic appliance—such as a TV, VCR, or dryer—that you use to do some task. The thrilling thing about a computer is that you can use it to do many types of tasks—write letters, draw a map, play a game, and more.

You don't really have to know a lot about how a computer works to use it. Think about your car. Your car works because of the different elements that make up the car: the engine, the transmission, the wheels, and so on. A PC is the same. It is actually a group of components working together.

Basically, a PC is the hardware—the physical components that you can see and touch—and the software—the programming instructions that make the physical components work.

WHAT IS HARDWARE?

The items that you unpack and actually touch are the hardware components. The hardware consists of the system box, monitor, keyboard, mouse, and other physical components. You learn more about hardware in the next lesson.

WHAT IS SOFTWARE?

Software consists of the program instructions that turn your PC into anything you want it to be. With the applicable software, you can use your PC to write letters, create reports, draw illustrations, make a presentation, balance your checkbook, and more. You can find many different types of software. Lesson 3 describes some basic types of applications.

WHAT CAN I DO WITH MY PC?

When you purchase a PC, you may have a clear-cut idea of what you want to use the PC for. You may want to be able to do work at home. You may want to provide a PC for your children to use. You may want to connect to the Internet. If you know why you bought a PC, you will probably have a easy time getting started. You can start with your main purpose and then add new skills as you get more proficient.

If you aren't sure why you got a PC in the first place, you may have to spend a little time thinking about what you want to do. The possibilities are pretty much endless. You can use the PC for a legitimate business purpose, for sheer fun, or both. Here are a few things you can do with a PC:

- **Create documents.** You can create memos, reports, newsletters, resumes, and more. Any document that you once created on a typewriter, you can now create on a PC.

- **Track your finances.** You can balance a budget, track your business or home expenses, calculate your taxes, and more.

- **Manage data.** You can keep track of clients, relatives, members, inventory, sales, events, and so on.

- **Draw.** You can create from simple to complex artwork using your PC and the appropriate drawing program.

- **Learn a new skill.** You can find programs that teach how to type, how to speak Spanish, how to cook, and more.

- **Play a game.** You can find all kinds of games. Just let your imagination take flight and fly a plane, conquer evil aliens, plan a city, play a game of chess, and more.

- **Connect to the Internet.** You learn more about the Internet in later lessons, but many people want a PC so that they can hook up to this network-of-networks and find all kinds of information without ever leaving their desk.

These are just a few types of things you can do. Really, you can use a PC to do just about anything. A friend that owned a training company called the company "So That's a PC" because eventually you will find that *one* thing that makes your life easier or more fun or more interesting. And you will say "so that's a PC!" Once you find that one thing, you will want to do more and more. If at one time you thought you hated computers, you *will* change your mind.

TYPES OF PCs

Basically, you can purchase two types of computers: an IBM or compatible, and a Macintosh. Around 80 percent of the computers sold are IBMs or compatibles, and usually the term PC refers to this type of computer. At one time, there used to be a difference in quality between an IBM and an IBM-compatible, but now you'll find the most popular PCs are IBM-compatibles. You can find companies like Dell, Gateway, Micron, and others that manufacture best-selling PCs.

Most PCs use Windows 95 (more about this topic in Lesson 3) or Windows NT (a networking version of Windows) as the operating system.

 Operating Systems An operating system is the software that enables your computer to work. You use the operating system to run and install programs, to manage files, and more.

A Macintosh differs from an IBM or IBM-compatible mainly because of the operating system. This type of computer uses a different operating system, called System 7. While you can share files from PCs to Macs, you cannot run programs created for Windows 95 on a Mac or vice versa. The Macintosh also uses a different microprocessor. (For information on microprocessors, see Lesson 4.)

Because IBM and compatibles are the primary PC market, this book covers this type of PC.

SYSTEM BOX TYPES

When discussing types of PCs, you may hear the term *tower model* or *desktop model*. This description refers to the style of the system box. A tower model sits upright on your floor (see Figure 1.1). A desktop model sits horizontally on your desk. The orientation of the system box is the only thing that is different; the components and how they work are the same.

LAPTOP AND NOTEBOOK COMPUTERS

If you want to use your PC in one spot like your home or office, you most likely have a desktop or tower model. If, on the other hand, you travel and want to take your PC with you, you may decide to purchase a portable PC.

With a portable PC, all of the elements are compacted and combined into one unit so that it is easy to carry. The difference between portable models is the size.

A *notebook* computer is about the size of a school notebook (10" × 12") and can weigh as little as four to six pounds (see Figure 1.2). You could fit a notebook PC in your briefcase. A *laptop* computer is similar to a notebook computer, but is bigger. It's usually thicker and weighs more.

FIGURE 1.1   System boxes come in different styles: desktop and tower models.

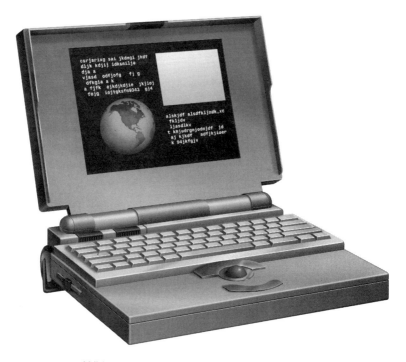

FIGURE 1.2   With a notebook PC, all of the components are compacted into one small case.

If you are thinking that smaller is less expensive, think again. Because a lot of complex technology is required to cram all of the components into a small package, most notebooks and laptops are more expensive than a comparable desktop system. If you *need* a notebook PC, then certainly get one. But if you don't really need one, you'll get more power and performance from a similarly priced desktop model.

In this lesson, you learned a basic definition of hardware and software as well as the different types of PCs. The next lesson discusses the key hardware components in more detail.

BASIC HARDWARE DEFINED

In this lesson, you learn about the basic hardware components of a PC.

A TYPICAL PC

When you purchase a PC, the following components are included:

- System unit
- Monitor
- Keyboard
- Mouse

This lesson describes these key elements as well as printers. Your PC may also include other elements like a modem or sound card. You can find more information on these hardware components in Lesson 6.

WHAT'S INSIDE THE SYSTEM BOX?

Probably the biggest element of your computer is the system box. This box houses all of the electronic wizardry that make up a PC. Here's what you would find if you opened up the box and took a look inside (see Figure 2.1):

- **Microprocessor.** The most important part of the computer is the microprocessor. You can think of this chip as the computer's "brain." The microprocessor is part of the motherboard (the main electronic board inside the

system unit) and determines the speed and features of a
PC. (You learn more about microprocessors in Lesson 4.)
Most everything hooks up to the motherboard.

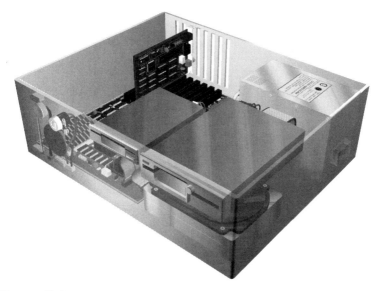

FIGURE 2.1   The system unit houses all the important electronic
components of the PC.

- **Memory.** When you run a program or create a document, the information is stored in memory, a temporary
  holding spot. Your computer has memory chips inside,
  housed on the motherboard. You learn more about
  memory in Lesson 4.

- **Disk drives.** You need a more permanent storage place
  for your data and programs, and this place is your hard
  drive. In addition to a hard drive, your system also probably has a floppy drive and possibly a CD-ROM drive. You
  learn all about drives in Lesson 5.

- **Power supply.** To power all of the elements inside the
  system box, you need a power supply. This box is housed
  inside the system unit, too.

- **Expansion slots.** So that you can add features to your PC, your system has expansion slots. You can insert electronic cards (sometimes called expansion cards) into these slots. Some slots may already be taken with such features as an internal modem or a sound card. For more information about extra elements, see Lesson 6.

LOOKING AT THE MONITOR

The monitor is the TV-like thing that you use to see what you are working on. The monitor displays programs on-screen. What you type also appears in the program window on the monitor. To use the monitor, flip the power switch. You may also make some adjustments to the display using the control knobs on the front of the monitor.

If you are more interested, you can read some background information to help you make sense of the different specifications you see advertised about monitors. This may help you better understand the type of monitor you have.

A monitor is actually two hardware components working together. You have the box that sits on your desk, and you have a video card inside the PC. The video card and motherboard are connected via a controller; and the video card and the monitor are connected via a plug on the back of the PC.

Monitors differ in a few key ways: size, quality of the image (or resolution), and the standard. The easiest thing to understand is the size. Monitors are measured diagonally like TVs. Most new monitors are usually 13" or bigger. (The bigger the monitor, the more you can see on-screen.)

Resolution, or the quality of the displayed image, is a little trickier. Computer monitors measure the number of pixels or dots per inch a monitor can display horizontally and vertically. You may see this as 640×480 or 1,024×768. With some monitors, you can select which resolution is used. The higher the number, the more dots per inch and the sharper the image.

Another monitor term you may hear is the *standard*. Most monitors today are VGA or SuperVGA. The standard controls the number of colors and resolution a particular monitor can display.

TYPING ON THE KEYBOARD

To enter information—type text, select commands—you use the keyboard. Most keyboards look about the same and have about the same number of keys. The most popular keyboard is the 101-key keyboard (see Figure 2.2).

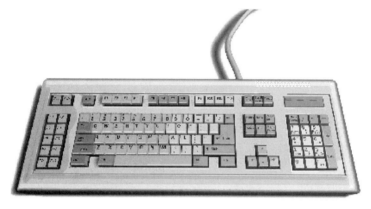

FIGURE 2.2 The 101-key keyboard includes alphanumeric keys, function keys, and cursor movement keys.

You use the keyboard like a typewriter: simply press the keys. In addition to alphanumeric characters, the keyboard also includes special keys you can use for shortcuts in programs. Different keys do different things depending on the program. For instance, pressing the F1 key in most programs displays the Help contents.

 Keyboard Stress   To avoid repetitive stress injuries sometimes associated with typing (such as carpal tunnel syndrome), you can buy a special type of keyboard designed to support your wrists while you type. Microsoft, for instance, sells this type of ergonomical keyboard.

Using a Mouse

Before Windows became the standard operating system, most commands were typed. Therefore, all you needed was a keyboard. Windows, because it is a graphical user interface, required an additional way to make choices. Windows enabled you to point to what you wanted. The input device for pointing and selecting is the mouse.

Now, the mouse is standard equipment on a PC. You can use the mouse to select menu commands, start programs, open windows, manipulate windows, and more.

Many beginners have trouble getting the hang of the mouse, but once you get some practice, you will find that it comes naturally. The following are the basic mouse moves:

- **Point.** To point to something on-screen, move the mouse on the desk until the pointer is in the spot you want.

- **Click.** To click, press the mouse button once. Most mice have more than one button. The left button is used most often. You may find some shortcuts which you can access by using the right mouse button.

- **Double-click.** To double-click, press the mouse button twice in rapid succession.

- **Drag.** To drag, click and hold down the mouse button and then drag the mouse. You use this dragging motion to select text, to move items, and to perform other tasks.

 Practice Makes Perfect   A good way to practice using the mouse is to play Solitaire. In this Windows card game, you can practice clicking and dragging until you get the "feel" of the mouse.

Many different companies manufacture mice, including Microsoft. The newest Microsoft mouse is called the Intellimouse and includes other features that software programs can take advantage of. For instance, many of the Microsoft Office programs use the Intellimouse for scrolling shortcuts.

PRINTING WITH THE PRINTER

When you purchase a new PC, you can expect that PC to include the system unit and all its contents, the monitor, the keyboard, and the mouse. This is a typical PC setup. In addition to these elements, you may also purchase a printer. You will most likely use your PC to create some type of document, and more often than not, you will want to print that document.

You can expect to find the following types of printers: dot-matrix printers, inkjet printers, and laser printers.

DOT-MATRIX PRINTERS

Dot-matrix printers used to be the most popular type of printer because they were the least expensive. As prices have dropped for other printer types, the popularity of this type of printer has declined. You may still find this printer, though, used for printing multi-part forms.

A dot-matrix printer works by firing a pin against a ribbon to make a dot on the page. The combination of dots form characters and graphics. In terms of quality, dot-matrix are at the bottom of the totem pole.

INKJET PRINTERS

You can think of inkjet printers as middle of the road. This type of printer doesn't offer the same quality as a laser printer, but it is better than a dot-matrix. They are usually in between the two in cost also.

An inkjet printer works by spraying tiny dots on a page through a tiny nozzle. The quality of the printout is usually pretty good, and the price is often reasonable. If you want a color printer, inkjet color printers are especially worth considering.

Laser Printers

A laser printer offers the fastest printing and better quality than any other printing. On the down side, it is usually a bit more expensive than other printer types. The price range and feature list of laser printers can vary greatly. You can find a simple, reasonably-priced desktop model or a big, fast, network printer.

In this lesson, you learned about the key hardware components that make up a typical PC. Turn to the next lesson for a basic primer on software.

3 LESSON

BASIC SOFTWARE DEFINED

In this lesson, you learn about the basic types of software.

WHAT IS AN OPERATING SYSTEM?

To handle the communication between the different hardware components, you need a system program. This program is called the operating system, and it handles such things as starting programs, storing files, printing documents, and so on.

All computers come with an operating system, and the most popular operating system is Windows 95. If you are using a network version of Windows, you may have Windows NT.

To use your computer, you do need to know a few things about Windows, and you can find some of the key Windows tasks in Lesson 9. Most of your time spent using your computer won't be spent actually in Windows; although Windows will be busy in the background handling all the behind-the-scenes type of work.

Most of your time spent using a PC will be spent using some type of application. The next section discusses the most popular types of applications.

TYPES OF APPLICATIONS

To perform a certain type of task using your computer—for instance, typing a letter—you need an application or program for that task. When you purchase a new PC, you may receive some applications as part of the purchase. Windows 95 also includes some mini-applications. These applications will get you started. You may also want to purchase additional applications as you learn to do more and more with your PC.

 What's In a Word?   You will hear the terms program, application, or some combination (application program) used interchangeably. They all mean the same thing.

WORD PROCESSORS

The most common type of application is word processing. You can use this type of program to create documents such as letters, memos, reports, manuscripts, and so on. If there was something you would have formally done on a typewriter, you now use a word processing program for the task.

Word processing programs are more than just a fancy typewriter, though. They offer many editing and formatting features so that you have a great deal of control over the content and look of your document. Here's a quick list of some of the things you can do with this type of program:

- **Easily edit text.** You can move text from one page to another, even one document to another. You can also copy or delete text with just a few keystrokes.

- **Format text.** Formatting means changing the appearance of text. You can make text bold, change the font, use a different color, and so on. Later in this chapter you learn how to make some formatting changes.

- **Format paragraphs and pages.** In addition to simple text changes, you can also format paragraphs (indent, add bullets, add a border) and pages (change the margins, add page numbers, insert a header).

- **Check accuracy.** Most programs include a spell-check program for checking the spelling. Some programs also include programs for checking grammar.

Word processing programs differ in what features they offer. If your needs are simple, you may do OK with the simple word processing program included with Windows. This program, called WordPad, includes basic editing and formatting features.

If you plan to create a lot of documents and want more control and features, you may want to purchase a more complete program. One of the most popular programs is Word for Windows, shown in Figure 3.1. This program includes all of the preceding features as well as desktop publishing features for setting up columns, inserting tables, adding graphics, and so on. Word for Windows also includes features for sending faxes, creating Web documents, and much more.

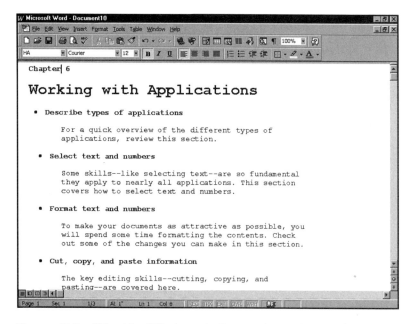

FIGURE 3.1   Word for Windows is the most popular word processing program.

If you want utmost control over the printed document, you may want to use—in addition to a word processing program—a desktop publishing program. These programs provide even more control of the layout of the page. Microsoft Publisher is a fairly simple desktop publishing program. PageMaker, on the other hand, is a more robust package.

SPREADSHEETS

If numbers are your game, then you will most likely work with a spreadsheet application. This type of program enables you to enter and manipulate all kinds of financial information: budgets, sales statistics, income, expenses, and so on. You enter these figures in a worksheet, a grid of columns and rows (see Figure 3.2). The intersection of a row and column is called a cell, and you enter text, numbers, or formulas into the cells to create a worksheet.

	A	B	E	G	I	K	L	M	N	O	P
1	My Budget										
2											
3		Budget	Jan Actual	Feb Actual	Mar Actual	Apr Actual					
4	Automobile	$ 462	$ 462	$ 462	$ 462	$ 462					
5	Books/CDs	$ 70	$ 79	$ 96	$ 22	$ -					
6	Cable	$ 30	$ -	$ -	$ 27	$ 27					
7	Cash	$ 80	$ -	$ -	$ 80	$ 80					
8	Charity	$ 130	$ 135	$ 100	$ 100	$ 150					
9	Child Care	$ 430	$ 525	$ 343	$ 420	$ 420					
10	Clothing	$ 200	$ 456	$ 338	$ 301	$ 582					
11	Furnishings	$ 50	$ -	$ -	$ -	$ 28					
12	Grocery	$ 450	$ 476	$ 294	$ 502	$ 329					
13	Gifts	$ 100	$ 142	$ 65	$ 154	$ 170					
14	Health Care	$ 80	$ 87	$ -	$ 17	$ 294					
15	Household	$ 220	$ 274	$ 261	$ 246	$ 53					
16	Housing	$ 50	$ -	$ 51		$ -					
17	Misc.	$ 50	$ 47	$ 611	$ 11	$ 18					
18	Utilities	$ 165	$ 196	$ 140	$ 201	$ 135					
19		$ 2,567	$ 2,879	$ 2,789	$ 2,543	$ 2,749					

FIGURE 3.2 Use a spreadsheet program for any type of numerical data you want to calculate or track.

The benefit of a spreadsheet program is that you have so many options for working with the data you enter. You can do any of the following:

- **Perform simple to complex calculations.** You can total a row of numbers, calculate a percentage, figure the amortization of a loan, and more.

- **Format the data.** You can make changes to how text and numbers appear in the worksheet. You can also adjust the column width, add borders, change the alignment of entries, and more.

- **Chart the data.** You can create different types of charts to visually represent the data. For instance, add a line chart to a report to illustrate a sales trend.

- **Manage data lists.** Most spreadsheets also include features for managing simple data lists. You can enter, sort, and query simple data lists using the grid structure of a worksheet.

Microsoft Excel for Windows, Lotus 1-2-3, and Quattro Pro are all popular spreadsheet programs.

In addition to spreadsheet programs, you can also use other types of financial programs. For example, you can purchase a program to keep track of your check register. One of the most popular check management programs is Quicken. You can also find programs for calculating your income tax, managing your small business, handling major accounting tasks, and so on.

DATABASES

If word processing and spreadsheets are the first two in application popularity, then databases round out the Big Three. You can use a database program to track and manage any set of data: clients, inventory, orders, events, and so on. Database programs vary from simple list managers to complex programs you can use to manage linked systems of information.

Databases offer a lot of advantages when you are working with large amounts of information. First, you can easily search for and find a particular piece of information. Second, you can sort the data into different orders as needed. Sort a client list alphabetically for a phone list. Sort by ZIP code for a mailing.

Third, you can work with subsets of the data: all clients in Indiana, all clients that ordered more than $10,000 worth of products, and so on.

Some popular database programs include Access, Approach, and Paradox.

GRAPHICS AND PRESENTATION PROGRAMS

Even if you aren't artistic, you can use your PC and the right software program to create graphics. Depending on your needs (and skill levels), you can consider any of the three types of programs in this category:

- **Simple drawing programs.** You can use a simple drawing program, such as Paint, which is included with Windows 95, to create simple illustrations.

- **Complex drawing programs.** You can also find more sophisticated programs for drawing and working with images. For instance, Adobe Illustrator and Adobe Photoshop are two such packages.

- **Presentation programs.** If you ever have to give a presentation, you may want to use a program designed just for creating presentations. You can use this program to create slides, handouts, and notes. Microsoft PowerPoint, Corel Presentations, and Freelance Graphics are popular presentation programs.

SUITES OR BUNDLES

One of the recent trends of software is to create a package or suite of the most popular programs and sell them together. For example, Microsoft offers several versions of Office, its suite of applications. The standard Office suite includes Word, Excel, PowerPoint, and Outlook. The professional edition adds Access. Corel and Lotus offer similar suites that include their most popular word processing, spreadsheet, database, and presentation programs.

PERSONAL INFORMATION MANAGERS

Most people have several things to keep track of: people, events, appointments, places, and so on. Personal information managers (or PIMs) are just the program for storing names and addresses, keeping track of your schedule, jotting jots, and so on. You can think of this type of program as your "electronic" day planner.

GAMES AND EDUCATIONAL SOFTWARE

Two other broad categories of software are games and educational software. Here, you will find a wealth and variety of programs. Learn how to cook, chart your family tree, play a card game, conquer another planet, learn French. The list goes on and on.

 Where To Start A good way to see what programs are available is to scan through the advertisements for software in a computer magazine.

INTERNET PROGRAMS

If you want to use your computer to hook up to the Internet, you need a browser. The two most popular are Netscape Communicator and Microsoft's Internet Explorer. You can find out more about what you need to connect to the Internet in Lesson 18.

UTILITY PROGRAMS

When you want to fine-tune your computer, you may want to investigate some of the utility programs that are available. These programs may add capabilities to your system such as virus checking, backing up, and so on.

In this lesson, you learned about the different types of applications. The next lesson goes into more depth about your hardware.

MEMORY AND THE PROCESSOR

In this lesson, you learn about two critical system components: the microprocessor and memory.

WHAT IS THE MICROPROCESSOR?

The most important part of a computer is the microprocessor chip, sometimes called the CPU (central processing unit) or simply processor. This tiny chip the size of a cracker determines the power of a computer. The two most important distinctions of the microprocessor are the name, or type, of chip and the speed.

THE TYPE OF CHIP

Originally, processor chips were named with numbers—the higher the number, the more powerful the chip. Here's a breakdown of the history of the microprocessor, from the earliest processor used in PCs to the newest:

8088	Used in the original IBM PC. Now obsolete.
8086	Used in the IBM PC XT. Now obsolete.
80286	Used in the AT computers. Now obsolete.
80386	Introduced and gained popularity in the late '80s. Now obsolete.
80486	Introduced in 1991. Now obsolete.
Pentium	Basically, a 80586 chip. Sometimes called the P5. Still sold today.

Pentium MMX	A Pentium chip with enhanced multi-media capabilities.
Pentium Pro	The newest generation of a Pentium. Basically, a 80686 chip or P6.
Pentium II	A Pentium Pro chip with MMX capabilities.

If you recently purchased a PC, you probably have a Pentium or Pentium MMX. If you have an older PC or a used PC, you may have a PC that uses an older chip. How can you tell? Look at the system box. Usually, you can find the processor type and speed (covered next) somewhere on the system box.

How Fast Is Your PC?

The speed of the chip is rated in megahertz (MHz). One megahertz equals one million clock ticks per second. The higher the megahertz, the faster the computer.

Most chips are available in different speeds, and you pay more for the faster computer. If you went shopping for a PC today, you could expect to find PCs at 120 MHz (slowest) to 200+ MHz (fastest). Again, the system box or the model name of your PC usually includes the speed. For instance, if you see P5-166, you have a 166 MHz Pentium processor.

Who Makes the Microprocessor?

You may see advertisements for Intel and even see an Intel logo on your PC. Intel does not make PCs, but does make microprocessors. For a long time, Intel dominated the PC chip market, but you can now find a few other companies that also manufacture microprocessor chips.

WHAT IS MEMORY?

After the microprocessor, the next most important component of
the computer is the amount of memory, or RAM, it has. RAM
stands for *random access memory* and is the working area of the
computer where the computer stores instructions and data. The
bigger the working area (i.e., more memory), the better.

RAM is measured in bytes. One kilobyte (abbreviated K or KB)
equals roughly 1,000 bytes. (One kilobyte actually equals 1,024
bytes, but the numbers are rounded.) One megabyte (abbreviated
M or MB) equals 1,000,000 bytes. One gigabyte (abbreviated G or
GB) equals one billion bytes. If you bought a new PC today, you
could expect to find PCs with anywhere from 16M to 48M or
more of RAM.

HOW MUCH MEMORY DO YOU HAVE?

It's easy to forget just how much memory your system has. If you
aren't sure, you can display the amount of memory (as well as the
processor type) by following these steps:

1. On the Windows desktop, right-click the My Computer
   icon.

2. From the shortcut menu that appears, select Properties.

   You see the System Properties dialog box which displays
   some information about your system (see Figure 4.1).

3. Click the Cancel button to close the dialog box.

ADDING MEMORY

One upgrade you can make to a PC is to add memory. Doing so
can improve the performance of your PC. Adding memory is a
fairly simple upgrade. The hardest part is figuring out what type
and size of memory chips your system takes. You can usually find
out this information by reviewing your system documentation or
by calling the PC manufacturer.

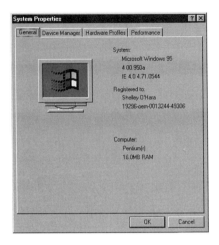

FIGURE 4.1   You can tell the processor type and amount of memory from this dialog box.

If you are buying a new PC, buy as much memory as you can! Memory is one feature worth spending extra money on. You can never have enough memory.

 Disk Cache   The computer can use some tricks to make it work faster, and one such trick is the use of a disk cache. The computer makes some assumptions about the information you use. If it thinks you are going to need certain information again, it *stashes* the information in a spot (called the cache) where the computer can quickly access it.

In this lesson, you learned about the microprocessor and memory, both critical in determining the speed and power of your PC. The next chapter covers another important hardware component—your disk drives.

DISK DRIVES

In this lesson, you learn about the different disk drives on a typical PC. Disk drives are important because you use them to store and move data.

WHAT DRIVES DO YOU HAVE?

Computers need a place to store information (files and programs) and that place is on a disk drive. When you save a file, the information is recorded magnetically onto the drive's surface. When you want to use that information again, the disk reads the information from the drive. On most new PCs, you can expect to have the following drive types:

- **Floppy drive.** If you take a close look at your system unit, you will notice a slot (like a little mail slot) on the front. This is the door to your floppy drive. To get data onto and off of your hard drive, you can use a floppy disk and drive.

- **Hard drive.** A hard drive is housed inside your system unit and is your main "cabinet" for storing data. You can read more about hard drives in the later section "What Is a Hard Drive?"

- **CD-ROM drive.** Newer PCs usually come with a CD-ROM drive as standard equipment; older computers may not have this type of drive.

Which drives do you have? A quick way to find out is to open My Computer. You should see drive icons for each of the drives on your system. Follow these steps:

1. Double-click the My Computer icon on the desktop. You see the contents of your system, including icons for each drive (see Figure 5.1). You also see some system folders.

FIGURE 5.1   Check out the drives on your PC by opening the My Computer icon.

2. Click the Close (X) button to close the window.

WHAT IS A FLOPPY DRIVE?

Your hard disk is the primary storage space for programs or files; therefore, you need a way to get programs onto the hard disk. What if you want to take a file with you—say take a file from your office PC to your home PC? A floppy disk drive provides the medium for moving information onto and off of your hard drive.

Older PCs used a different type of floppy drive. The disks were 5 1/4" in size and were actually floppy. As technology advanced, a new type of floppy disk became popular. This type of disk is 3 1/2" in size and is encased in hard plastic.

Disks vary in the amount of information they can store (called the *capacity*). The capacity is measured in megabytes (M) or kilobytes (K). You can find 5 1/4" disks in 360K and 1.2M size. The 3 1/2" disks come in two capacities: 720K and 1.44M. If you have a 3 1/2" drive (and that's all most new computers come with), you can use either the 720K or the 1.44M disk.

If you have a fairly new PC, you probably have just one floppy disk, and it is probably a 3 1/2" drive. Drives have names, and if you have one drive, your floppy drive is named Drive A. Older PCs may have two floppy drives: Drive A and Drive B.

The Future of Floppies   As technology advances, newer types of floppy disks are emerging. You can, for instance, purchase a Zip drive. This type of disk and drive can store even more information than the standard 3 1/2" floppy disk and drive.

INSERTING AND EJECTING DISKS

To insert a disk into the drive, slide it into the drive (label up) until you hear a click. To eject a disk, press the disk drive button.

FORMATTING A FLOPPY DISK

Before you can use a floppy disk, you must prepare it for use, and this process is called *formatting*. Formatting divides the disk up into storage units, where the data will be saved. You can purchase preformatted floppy disks to save time. If you did not purchase preformatted disk or you want to format an existing disk, you can do so using Windows 95.

 Be Aware!   Formatting erases all of the information on a disk. If you are formatting an existing disk, be sure the disk does not contain any information that you need.

To format a disk, follow these steps:

1. Insert the disk you want to format into the drive.

2. Double-click the My Computer icon on the Windows desktop.

3. Right-click your floppy drive (usually Drive A) and select the Format command. You see the Format dialog box (see Figure 5.2).

FIGURE 5.2   Use this dialog box to format a floppy disk.

4. If necessary, display the Capacity drop-down list and select the correct capacity for your disk.

5. Select the type of format. Quick formats the disk and erases all of the files; this method does not check the disk for bad sectors. Full erases the files, prepares the disk, and checks for bad sectors. Copy System Files Only adds the system files to the disk so that you can use this disk to start your PC.

6. If you want, enter a label into the Label text box.

7. Click the Start button.

8. When you see a message telling you the format is complete, click the OK button.

Once the floppy is formatted, you can use it to store files. You can copy files from your hard drive, discussed in the next section, to your floppy disk.

WHAT IS A HARD DRIVE?

All PCs come with a hard disk, and you store your programs and data files on this hard disk. The hard disk is housed inside the system unit. Most systems have just one hard disk, but you can always add another—either another internal drive housed in the system unit or an external drive that is connected to the PC via a cable.

Like the floppy drive, the hard drive has a name, and it is usually Drive C.

How Drives Differ

Drives differ in a few key ways. The most important distinction is size (again, called the capacity). Hard drives are measured in megabytes (M) or gigabytes (G). The bigger the drive, the better. You will be surprised how fast your drive fills up with programs and files!

Drives also differ in how fast they are—that is, how fast the drive takes to find and access information. The speed is measured in milliseconds (ms). Anything in the 8–12 ms range is a good speed.

The microprocessor and hard drive communicate to each other via a controller, and drives differ in the type of controller they use. Here's a quick breakdown of the different controller types:

Name	Description
IDE	Stands for Integrated Device Electronics. An older, but decent controller. Mostly now replaced by EIDE.
SCSI	Stands for Small Computer Systems Interface. A controller that enables you to chain different devices together.
EIDE	Stands for Enhanced Integrated Device Electronics. A newer version of the IDE controller.

What Size Is Your Hard Disk?

When you first purchased your PC, you probably knew the size of the drive; but after you've had your PC a while, you may not

remember the size. You also may want to review how much space
is taken and how much space is free. You can quickly review this
and other hard drive information using Windows 95. Follow
these steps:

1. Double-click the My Computer icon on the desktop.

2. Right-click the icon for your hard drive.

3. From the submenu that appears, select Properties. You see
    the Properties dialog box, shown in Figure 5.3. You can
    see the capacity of the drive, the space used, and the
    space free.

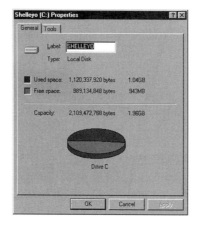

FIGURE 5.3 Review drive information using this dialog box.

4. Review the information and then click the OK button.

In addition to a hard drive, you may also have a CD-ROM drive,
and this type of drive is covered next.

WHAT IS A CD-ROM DRIVE?

Floppy disks can only store so much information; therefore, a
newer method for distributing information emerged: CD-ROM
discs. These discs can store much more information than a regular

floppy disk; they can store over 700M of data. But while you can both read and write information to a floppy disk, you can only read the data from a CD-ROM. (ROM stands for Read-Only Memory.)

CD-ROMs became popular and standard equipment on PCs when multimedia became popular. Multimedia programs combine text, video, graphics, and sound; and because video, graphic, and sound files are really big, CD-ROM discs became ideal for distributing information like programs, encyclopedias, and other large collections of information.

If you have a newer PC, you most likely have a CD-ROM drive as part of your system. Usually this drive is housed inside the system unit, and like other drives has a name. If you have just one hard drive, your CD-ROM drive is most likely Drive D.

CD-ROM drives differ in their speed. You often see the speed advertised as 8X; that's eight times as fast as the original drive's speed. Speed measurements like 8X or 6X can be arbitrary. If you really want to know the speed, find out the access time and transfer time.

To insert a disc into the drive, you press the Eject button and then lay the disc inside the drive. Press the drive door to insert the disc. Some drives have a cartridge. Insert the disc into the cartridge and then insert the cartridge into the drive.

 CDs Everywhere!   New versions of CD drives are becoming available that enable you to both read and write data to a CD disc.

In this lesson, you learned about the different types of drives on a PC. The next lesson continues the discussion of hardware, covering some of the other hardware components you might have.

6

L E S S O N

ADD ONS:
EXTRA
HARDWARE

In this lesson, you learn about some additional hardware components you may have on your PC.

MODEMS

Your PC may include a modem. Why have a modem? Because you can use a modem (and a phone line) to hook up to online services such as America Online and to connect to the Internet. You can send and receive e-mail messages, visit Web pages, participate in online discussion groups, and more. (You can learn more about the Internet in Lessons 18–21.)

You may have either an internal modem that is housed inside the system unit, or an external modem that sits on your desk and is connected to your PC via a cable.

To use a modem, you plug the phone line into the appropriate jack on the modem.

HOW A MODEM WORKS

The computer creates and works with digital information (on and off switches, or 0s and 1s). A phone line, on the other hand, transmits information using analog signals (or sound waves). That's where the modem comes in. Modem stands for *MOdulator-DEModulator*, which means it translates the digital information to analog and sends the analog information over the phone lines. The receiving modem then translates the analog information back to digital.

DO YOU NEED A SEPARATE PHONE LINE?

You need a phone line, then, to hook up to the online world. You can use your existing phone, but then you have to coordinate when the line is used for the PC and when the line is used for phone calls. Doing so may be a bother, and you may want to install a second line specifically for your modem. You can have another line hooked up by calling your phone company.

HOW FAST IS YOUR MODEM?

When you are using the telephone line or hooked up to an online service, you are usually charged for the time you are connected. The shorter the time, the less expensive the charge. Therefore, you want a modem that can connect and transmit data quickly.

Modem speed is measured in bits per second (Bps) or kilobytes per second (Kbps). (You may hear the term *baud* which is often used to mean Bps.) Common speeds for today's modems are 28,800 (or 28.8 Kbps) and 33,600 (or 33.6 Kbps). You can also find some 56 Kbps modems.

 The Need For Speed The existing phone lines can only handle up to a certain speed (about 56 Kbps). Also, you may be limited in speed by the provider you use to connect to the Internet. You can read more about service providers in Lesson 19.

A COMBINATION FAX/MODEM

In addition to a plain modem, you can also purchase a fax modem. Using your computer and a fax modem, you can send and receive faxes over the phone line.

With a fax modem, you create the document you want to fax on the computer. Then using the fax modem, you can send this document over the phone lines to any type of fax machine (not

just computer fax modems). Your computer can also receive faxes.
You can view them on-screen or have them printed directly to
your printer.

 What About Paper? Keep in mind that you can't fax
paper copies using a fax modem; you can send only
documents created using the computer.

SOUND CARDS AND SPEAKERS

Another hardware component you may have (or consider adding)
is a sound card. A sound card is an electronic card housed inside
the system unit; it is inserted in an expansion slot inside your PC.
You then hook up speakers to the sound card.

With a sound card, you can play and hear sounds. Where do you
find these sounds? Many multimedia programs include sounds.
For instance, if you have a multimedia encyclopedia (sold on CD-
ROM), you can look up entries for say Martin Luther King and
play back his famous "I Have a Dream" speech.

Many games include sound effects. You can also record and include sound message in a document. Also, as you explore the
Internet, you will find sound files, such as interviews, new music
clips, and other audio information.

And yes, you can play your audio CDs on your computer's CD-
ROM drive. To do so, you can use the CD Player program included with Windows 95. Lesson 15 describes this and other
sound features of Windows 95.

OTHER DRIVES

If you use your PC for business, you will want to be sure to set up
a backup routine. A backup makes an extra copy of your data so
that if something happens to the original, you can use the backup
copy. To save time backing up, you may have purchased a special
type of tape backup unit.

A floppy disk can store only so much information. If you work with large documents—graphics, sound, and video documents are usually huge—you may want to try the new Zip drives by Iomega. These drives are similar to a floppy drive, but the disks can store much more information. Many new PCs offer a Zip drive as an optional upgrade.

Finally, new CD-R (CD Recordable) drives are becoming available. With this type of drive, you can not only read information from a CD disc, but also write data to the disc.

SCANNERS

If you are an artist or have an interest in creating artwork, you may consider adding a scanner to your PC. A scanner converts a printed image into an electronic image so that you can manipulate the image on the PC. For example, you can scan in photographs, illustrations, and documents.

A flat-bed scanner works like a photocopier. A hand-held scanner works by moving the scanner over the image.

JOYSTICKS

Play a lot of games? If so, a joystick might be on your PC upgrade list. Some games, especially arcade-style games, are easier to play with a joystick. You plug a joystick into one of the ports at the back of your PC. You can then use the joystick controls to jump, punch, shoot, dodge, and so on, depending on your game of choice.

In this lesson, you learned about some additional hardware you may have or consider adding to your PC. The next lesson tells you how to set up all this hardware.

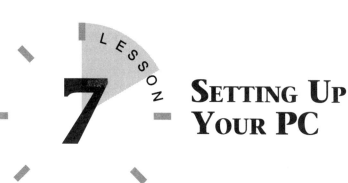

7

LESSON

SETTING UP YOUR PC

In this lesson, you learn how to set up a PC.

PICKING A GOOD WORKSPACE

If you already have your PC set up, you may want to skim this lesson to see if you can pick up any pointers. If you just purchased a new PC, you can read this chapter to figure out how to set up all the components. The first step is to find a good workspace, and that requires a little planning.

DO YOU HAVE ENOUGH DESK SURFACE?

You need a flat surface (usually a desk) for your monitor, keyboard, and mouse. If you have a desktop system, you also need a spot for the PC. You can stack the monitor on top of the system unit if you want.

If you have a sound card and speakers, you need a spot for your speakers. And finally, don't forget your printer. All of these elements are connected to the PC via cables, so they have to be close to the system unit.

If you have a tower system (the PC sits on the floor), you need to pick a spot for the system unit that is close enough to the desktop items. Remember everything plugs into the back of the PC.

Don't forget that you also need some space to work. You will want some place where you can lay out papers and write on your desk too.

Is Power Close By?

The system unit, monitor, and printer need to be plugged into an outlet, so you need a power source close by. You might want to purchase a surge protector. Not only can you plug all of the components into this power strip, but the surge protector can protect against power surges, which can damage data and your PC.

 Watch Out!   Surge protectors cannot protect from lightning. In severe weather, unplug the entire system from the power and the telephone lines to avoid damage to your PC.

Keep in mind that not all power supplies/surge protectors are the same. A surge protector outlet strip gives you surge protection and has a specific rating for surges. Also these types usually have a guarantee from the manufacturer that if your equipment is damaged, they will reimburse a "flat" monetary rate. These also can provide protection for a telephone line.

You can also purchase a power conditioning unit, such as an American Power Conversion UPS backup. These not only have a "circuit breaker" to cut the circuit when a large surge is detected, but will also provide a DC battery backup when the power is out and will allow the computer to continue to operate for a period of time (usually around 15 minutes). Be sure you get one that offers protection against power surges and not just a plain old power supply.

Is a Phone Jack Nearby?

If you have a modem and plan on using it to connect to the Internet or other online services, you need a phone line connection. This is another consideration as you plan where to put your PC.

CAN YOU TYPE COMFORTABLY?

When deciding where to place your keyboard, keep in mind that you want your wrists flat as you type. If you bend them up or down, you run the risk of injury. You can purchase computer desks that have a separate, pull-out shelf for the keyboard.

 Do Not Bend Be sure the keyboard enables you to type properly. If you have to bend your wrists, you can develop a repetitive stress injury like carpal tunnel syndrome.

CAN YOU SEE THE MONITOR OK?

Be sure that you can comfortably view the monitor. You don't want the monitor too close or too far. Also, check the height of the monitor. You don't want to strain your neck, so be sure the monitor is at eye level.

In addition, if you place the computer in a room with windows, check for glare on the monitor. Remember to check during different times of the day to avoid early morning or late afternoon glare from the sun.

 No Glare You can also purchase anti-glare filters for your monitor.

UNPACKING THE PC

Once you have picked the spot, you can unpack your system unit. Be sure to save all of the documentation and paperwork included with the PC. Keep all of this information in one spot.

You should also save your boxes in case you need to ship your system. If there's a problem with your PC, you may need to ship it back to the manufacturer in the original packing. The boxes are also handy if you move or need to ship your PC for some other reason.

After you get everything unpacked, set up the components in your work area. The next step is connecting all of the parts.

MAKING ALL THE CONNECTIONS

Your computer should have come with complete instructions on what connections you need to make. On all PCs, you make some basic connections (the monitor, keyboard, and mouse). Depending on the equipment you have, you may need to make other connections. For instance, if you have a sound card, you need to hook up your speakers.

All of the connections are made to the back of the PC which, as you can see in Figure 7.1, has various types of connectors. You have to match up each connector to the appropriate cable. If you are lucky, each connector is labeled or color coded. If not, you can refer to your system documentation for help.

Here are the basic connections you need to make:

- Connect the video cable from the monitor to the monitor connector on the back of the PC.

- Connect the keyboard cable to the keyboard connector on the back of the PC.

- Connect the mouse cable to the mouse connector on the back of the PC.

- Connect the printer to the printer port on the back of the PC. Most printers connect to the parallel or LPT1 port. If you have a serial printer, you connect to one of the serial ports.

- Connect the power cord for the monitor to the back of the monitor. The other end will plug into the power source.

- Connect the power cord for the PC to the back of the PC. The other end will plug into the power source.

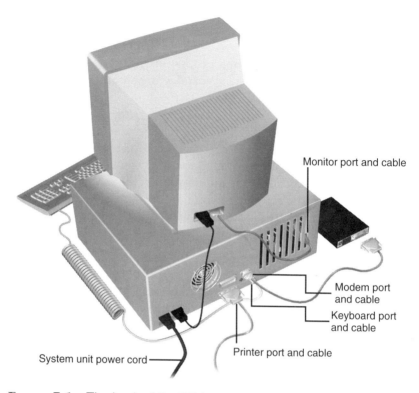

Monitor port and cable

Modem port
and cable

Keyboard port
and cable

System unit power cord

Printer port and cable

FIGURE 7.1 The back of the PC has connectors for each hardware component you need to hook up.

Size Counts If you can't figure out which is which, you can count the pins. A printer port has 25 pins. A standard serial port on current retail computers has nine pins, and a VGA monitor port has 15 pins.

You may also need to hook up speakers to the sound card. The speakers may also have a separate power connection. Check your manual.

If you have an internal modem, the back of the PC also contains jacks for plugging in your phone line. Make any other connections.

Plugging It In

Once you've got all the connections made, plug in the monitor and plug in the PC power. Turn on the monitor and then the PC. You are set and ready to go! Turn to the next lesson for information on starting up your PC.

 Nothing Happen?   If nothing happens when you turn on the PC, be sure that the power cables are plugged in. If you are using a surge protector, be sure that it is turned on.

Storing Your Manuals

As mentioned previously, it's a good idea to keep all of the boxes for your system. You should also keep all the paper work together—invoice, warranties, software certificates, receipts, and so on. Also, look for a place for all the system documentation. You may need to refer to the documentation for setup and to troubleshoot any problems that pop up.

In this lesson, you learned how to set up a PC. The next lesson explains starting, resetting, and shutting down a PC.

STARTING UP YOUR PC

In this lesson, you learn how to start, reset, and shut down your PC.

TURNING ON THE PC

After all the connections are made, you can plug in the system unit and monitor, and flip the power switches to start the PC. You should see some information flash across the screen as your system goes through its startup routine. For instance, you may see the results of a memory check. You may see setup commands for your hardware. After the system starts up, you should see Windows 95 (or whatever operating system you have on your PC).

Windows 95 starts automatically each time you turn on your PC. The next section describes what you see on the typical Windows desktop.

If nothing happens when you turn on your PC, check the following:

- Do both the PC and the monitor have power?

- Are all the components connected?

- Did you turn on both the monitor and the PC? They each have separate power buttons.

- Do you need to adjust the monitor? The monitor includes buttons for controlling the brightness of the display. It's easy to think the monitor isn't working when in fact you just can't see anything because of the brightness or other settings. Check these controls.

UNDERSTANDING THE WINDOWS DESKTOP

When you start your PC, you see the Windows desktop, shown in Figure 8.1. This is always your starting place, and like your physical desktop, the Windows desktop includes several tools to get you started. Each of these items are placed on the *desktop* (the background area).

Start button   My Computer icon   Recycle Bin icon   Desktop   Taskbar

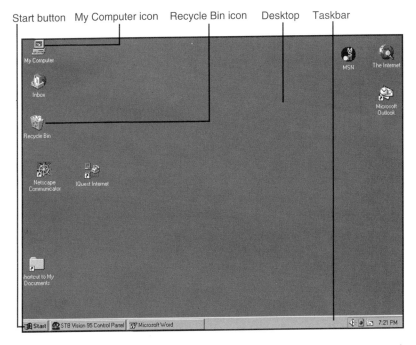

FIGURE 8.1   The Windows desktop includes a taskbar, icons, and a Start button.

ICONS

You can place different items on the desktop so that they are always available. Each item is represented by a little picture called an icon. (You learn more about adding items to the desktop in Lesson 16.) Windows includes several icons by default.

 Icons An icon is a picture that represents something like a file, program, folder, printer, or disk.

The My Computer icon is used to display the contents of your PC. You learn more about using this icon in Lesson 14, "Managing Your Files."

The Recycle Bin icon is used to store files, folders, and programs you have deleted. Lesson 14 explains all about deleting and undeleting files.

You may have several other icons. For instance, if you are hooked up to a network, you may see the Network Neighborhood icon, which you can use to access and display the contents of the network.

You may have icons for programs. My desktop, for instance, includes icons for programs that I frequently use. You may have icons for setting up MSN (The Microsoft Network), a folder for online services, or an icon for your Inbox.

THE START BUTTON

The place where the action is in Windows 95 is the Start button. You use this button to start programs, get help, and access commands for customizing Windows with the Control Panel. To display the Start menu, click the Start button (see Figure 8.2).

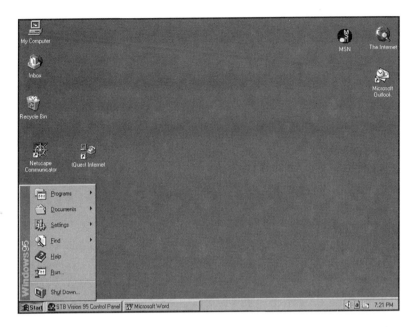

FIGURE 8.2   When you click the Start button, you see commands for starting programs, opening documents, getting help, and more.

THE TASKBAR

The Start button is the first item in the taskbar, the horizontal bar along the bottom of the desktop. This button also includes buttons for each window you have open or program you have running, which makes it easy for you to see what you have open. More importantly, the taskbar is what you use to switch among different programs.

If you work with more than one program, you may want to switch from one to the other. Windows 95's taskbar makes it easy. To switch to another program or window, simply click the button for that program or window in the taskbar. That program or window becomes active.

The taskbar also displays the current time and status icons for different tasks such as printing, e-mail, and so on.

The Time of Day   To display the current date, put the mouse pointer on the time. The date pops up. To change the date or time, double-click the date and then make any changes in the dialog box that appears.

You can change the placement and look of the taskbar. For more information on these changes, see Lesson 16.

WHAT TO DO IF YOU DON'T SEE THE WINDOWS DESKTOP

It's more than likely that you have Windows 95 on your PC; but if you don't see the Windows desktop shown in the preceding section, your system may have a different setup.

One possibility is that you have a different operating system. You can refer to your system documentation about how to use the operating system on your PC.

Another possibility is that you have another desktop manager working on top of Windows 95. I've seen this on some new PCs. The manufacturer adds a layer over Windows 95 (a shell that runs on top of Windows), with its own set of windows and controls and icons for using the PC. Personally, I think this makes using the PC more difficult. Each setup is different, so you can't ask others for help or really use a general-purpose book like this one. If this is the case, I'd recommend looking in your system documentation and figuring out how to turn off the desktop manager and just use Windows. Usually the shell is loaded from the Startup menu, and you can disable it by removing it from this folder.

RESTARTING YOUR PC

Using a PC isn't error-proof. Sometimes things happen that make the PC freeze up. For instance, a program may crash. When this happens, pressing the keys does nothing. The PC just won't respond. In this case, you can restart your PC.

TRY THESE THINGS FIRST!

If your system won't respond, check a few things. First, check to
see if the disk activity light is blinking. You can find this button
on the front of the PC. If the light is blinking or you hear sounds,
the PC may be busy saving a file or handling some other activity.
Wait a few minutes.

Second, be sure you know where you are. It's easy to switch to a
different program, say back to the Windows desktop, without
intending to. You think you are typing in your word processing
program, but you are really back at the desktop, and Windows 95
doesn't understand all that typing. Try clicking in the program
window or using the taskbar to make sure you are in the program
you think you are.

Third, check the screen. As another example, you may have
opened a menu or dialog box without realizing it. Again, if you
try typing, all you may hear are beeps. Try pressing Esc (the Escape key) to close any open menus or dialog boxes.

RESTARTING THE PC

If all else fails, you can restart your PC. First, try the menu command:

1. Click the Start button and select Shut Down. You see the
    Shut Down Windows dialog box (see Figure 8.3).

FIGURE 8.3   Select whether you want to restart or shut down
Windows.

2. Select Restart the Computer.

3. Click the Yes button.

If you can't click to get the Start menu open, you have to use a
different method. Try the keyboard method: Press and hold down
the Ctrl key. Then press Alt and Delete. You often see this abbreviated as Ctrl+Alt+Delete.

If the keyboard method doesn't work, press the Reset button on
the front of the PC. And if that doesn't work, or if you don't have
a Reset button, try turning the PC off and then on.

 What About DOS?   If you need to install a DOS program, you can restart your PC in MS-DOS mode by selecting Restart in MS-DOS mode. Many games, for
instance, are DOS programs and are installed and run
from MS-DOS mode.

SHUTTING DOWN THE PC

Windows 95 takes care of all the background details of using your
PC—things like storing files, handling the printer, and so on.
Because it is often busy in the background, you shouldn't just
turn off your PC. Instead, use the proper shutdown procedure so
that Windows can take care of any housekeeping tasks before
turning off the power.

Follow these steps to shut off your PC properly:

1. Click the Start button and select Shut Down. You see the
   Shut Down Windows dialog box (refer to Figure 8.3).

2. Select Shut Down the Computer.

3. Click the Yes button.

When you see a message saying that it is safe to turn off your PC,
you can turn it off.

In this lesson, you learned the proper way to start, restart, and
shut down your PC. Turn to the next lesson for some help on key
Windows tasks.

Using Windows 95

9

In this lesson, you learn some key skills for working with Windows.

UNDERSTANDING THE START BUTTON

Probably the most important item on the Windows desktop is the Start button. Not only do you use this to start programs, but also to access most Windows 95 features and commands.

To display the Start menu, click the Start button. You see the following choices (see Figure 9.1):

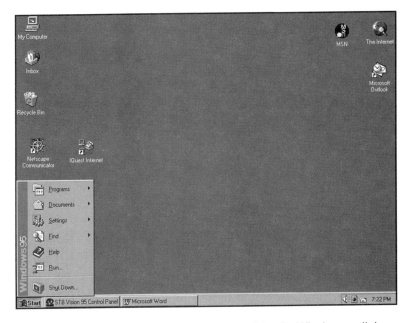

FIGURE 9.1 When you want to do something in Windows, click the Start button to begin.

- **Programs.** Use this command to start a program. Programs are organized into folders, displayed as submenus on the Programs menu. You learn more about starting programs in the next lesson.

- **Documents.** Use this command to open a document you just recently worked on. This method for starting a program and opening a document is also covered in the next lesson.

- **Settings.** Use this command to access the Control Panel, Taskbar, and Printers folders, which you can use to set up and customize different Windows components. Customizing is the topic of Lesson 16.

- **Find.** Use this command to search for files on the PC. Finding files is covered in Lesson 14.

- **Help.** Use this program to get online help, as covered later in this lesson.

- **Run.** Use this command to run programs, usually done for installing new programs. You can read about installing programs in Lesson 12.

- **Shut Down.** Use this command to shut down the computer before you turn off the power. Lesson 8 explained how to perform this task.

SELECTING COMMANDS FROM WINDOWS 95

You can select commands from Windows 95 in two ways: from the Start menu and from shortcut menus.

SELECTING COMMANDS FROM THE START MENU

To select a command from the Start menu, follow these steps:

1. Click the Start button. You see the top-level menu commands.

2. To display a submenu, put the pointer over the command you want to select. You can also click the command. When the pointer is over a command with a submenu (indicated with an arrow), the submenu is displayed. Continue selecting commands from submenus by pointing to them until you get to the selection you want.

3. Click your selection.

The command is carried out. For instance, if you select a program icon, that program is started.

USING SHORTCUT MENUS

In addition to the main commands in the Start menu, Windows 95 uses several shortcut menus. You can display these menus and select commands by using the right mouse button. Follow these steps:

1. Point to the item you want to work with. You can display a shortcut menu for the desktop, the taskbar, icons, files, the time in the status bar, and other "hot" spots.

2. Click the right mouse button. This is often called right-clicking. A shortcut menu is displayed. Figure 9.2 shows the shortcut menu for the desktop. You can use these commands to modify how the desktop appears.

3. Click the command you want.

WORKING WITH WINDOWS

Everything in Windows is displayed in a window, and one of the key skills you need to learn is how to manipulate a window—that is, how to open, close, resize, and move a window. This section covers these key skills.

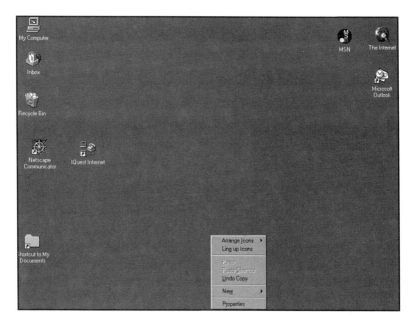

FIGURE 9.2 You can display shortcut menus for on-screen items like the desktop.

OPENING A WINDOW

Some windows display the contents of a disk or folder. For instance, the My Computer icon displays the contents of your system and the Recycle Bin displays the contents of this folder. To open this type of window, double-click the icon. The window is displayed on the desktop, and you also see a button for the window in the taskbar.

Some windows display a program. To open this type of window, start the program (covered in the next lesson). The program is started and displayed in a program window, and Windows adds a button for this program to the taskbar.

Both types of windows have the same set of controls. Figure 9.3 shows the contents of My Computer in a window.

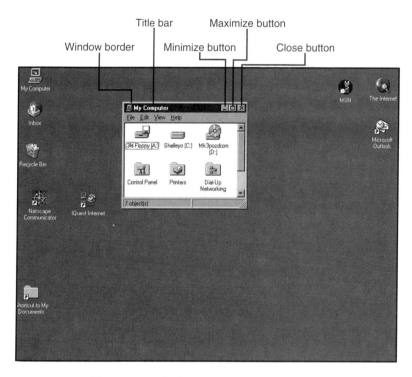

FIGURE 9.3   To open a window, double-click the icon. This is the result.

 Windows and Controls   One thing that can be confusing for beginners is that when you are working in a program, you actually have two windows open: the program window and the document window. Each has its own set of controls. The set in the title bar controls the program window. The set below this one (to the far right of the menu bar when the document window is maximized) controls the document window.

CLOSING A WINDOW

To close a window, click the Close (X) button in the title bar. If you close a program window, you exit that program.

Shortcut You can also close programs or windows by right-clicking the button for that program or window on the taskbar. From the shortcut menu, select the Close command.

RESIZING A WINDOW

You may have several windows open at the same time. To view them all, you may need to make some adjustments to the windows size. You have a lot of options for resizing. You can use the buttons in the title bar, or you can drag the window borders. For resizing, do any of the following:

- To minimize a window (shrink it to a button on the taskbar), click the Minimize button. When you minimize a window, that window or program is still running, but is not displayed in a window.

- To maximize a window (expand it to fill the entire screen), click the Maximize button. When a window is maximized, the window does not have borders, so you cannot resize by dragging the border. Also, the Maximize button becomes the Restore button.

- To restore a maximized window to its original size, click the Restore button.

- To resize a window, put the pointer on any of the window's borders, but not on the title bar. Drag the border to change the size of the window.

Moving a Window

If you have several windows open, you may also need to move windows around to see just what you want. You can move a window by following these steps:

1. Put the pointer on the title bar.

2. Drag the window to the location you want.

 The Arrangement You can have Windows arrange all windows on-screen. To do so, right-click a blank area of the taskbar and then select Cascade, Tile Horizontally, or Tile Vertically. Cascade displays the windows on top of each other; you can see the title bar of each window. Tile Horizontally displays each window in horizontal panes. Tile Vertically displays each window in vertical panes.

Getting Help

You really can't be expected to remember each command and feature of Windows. You will find that you will remember the day-to-day stuff, the tasks you perform all the time. But for less often used tasks, you may need a little reminder. You can use online help for these tasks.

You can use online help to look up a topic in one of three ways: using the table of contents, using the Help index, or searching for a Help topic.

Using Help Contents

Follow these steps to look up a topic in the table of contents:

1. Click the Start button and select the Help command. The Help Topics dialog box appears.

2. If necessary, click the Contents tab. Windows displays the Contents tab, which contains a list of topics, each represented by a book icon. You can open any of these topics.

3. Double-click any of the book topics. Windows displays additional subtopics. Do this until you see a help "page." Help pages are indicated with question mark icons (see Figure 9.4).

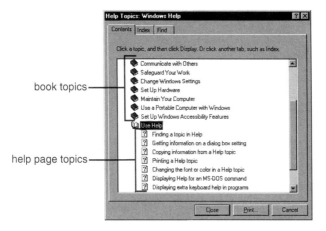

FIGURE 9.4   You can look up topics in the table of contents.

4. Double-click the help page. A help window appears, giving detailed information about the selected topic.

5. When you are finished reading the help information, close the window by clicking the Close button.

Browsing the table of contents is good when you want some general advice. When you are looking for something specific, you can use a different method—the index, for instance.

USING THE HELP INDEX

If you can't find the topic in the table of contents, you can also try looking up a topic using the index. Follow these steps:

1. Click the Start button and select the Help command.

2. In the Help Topics dialog box, click the Index tab.

3. In the first text box, type the first few letters of the topic for which you want help. Windows displays matching topics in the list box.

4. Double-click the topic you want. Windows displays the help information for the selected topic.

5. When you finish reading this information, close the window by clicking the Close button.

The index includes many topics, all listed alphabetically. In addition to this method, you can also search for a help topic, covered next.

SEARCHING FOR A HELP TOPIC

If you can't find a topic by browsing the table of contents or looking it up in the index, you can search for a topic. Follow these steps:

1. Click the Start button and select the Help command.

2. In the Help Topics dialog box, click the Find tab.

 First Timers   If this is the first time you've used Find, the Find Setup wizard appears. Click Next, then Finish. The wizard creates a word list for searching.

3. In the first text box, type the word or words that you want to find. Windows displays matching topics in the list box.

4. To narrow the search, click the matching topic that is closest to what you are looking for. Windows displays the topics that contain the word or words you typed.

5. Double-click the topic you want.

6. When you finish reading this information, close the window by clicking the Close button.

In this lesson, you learned some key skills for working with Windows 95. The next lesson explains how to start a program.

WORKING WITH PROGRAMS

*In this lesson, you learn how to start
a program.*

FIGURING OUT WHAT PROGRAMS YOU HAVE

When you get a new system, you might not even know what you
have and what you don't. It's confusing for beginners to get a
new PC and wonder "where did I get that?." You can review this
section to help you get a clue about what programs your system
contains.

You can expect to find three types of programs: Windows 95 programs, programs that came pre-installed on your system, and
programs that you've installed yourself.

WINDOWS 95 PROGRAMS

Windows 95 includes several different programs which are set up
when Windows is installed. You can expect to find the following
programs:

- **Accessory programs.** You can find these programs in
  the Accessories folder on the Program menu. Expect to
  find folders for Games; Multimedia programs (CD Player,
  Media Player, Sound Recorder, Volume Control); and
  System Tools (programs for backing up your system,
  defragmenting your hard drive, etc.). You also have icons
  for these programs: Calculator, Dial-Up Networking,
  HyperTerminal, Notepad, Paint, Phone Dialer, and
  Wordpad.

- **MS-DOS prompt.** Use this program to access the MS-DOS prompt for working with files, installing DOS programs, and doing other DOS tasks.

- **Windows Explorer.** Use this program to work with the files on your system.

- **Control Panel programs.** You find these programs by clicking the Start button, selecting Settings, and then selecting Control Panel. You learn more about these tools for customizing Windows in Lesson 16.

 The Set Up Depending on how Windows was installed, not all of these programs may have been set up. You can add Windows components, as covered in Lesson 12.

PRE-INSTALLED PROGRAMS

Your system may also have come with some software as part of the purchase. What you received will vary depending on not only the manufacturer of your PC, but also the model you purchased. For instance, if you purchased a "family" PC, you may have received some entertainment and home software (encyclopedia, games, etc.). If you purchased a "business" PC, you may have received some business software like Microsoft Office. Usually this software comes pre-installed.

You can usually tell what software is set up on your system by opening the Start menu and selecting Programs. You see the program folders and icons on your system. You can also check your system documentation.

PROGRAMS YOU'VE INSTALLED

Your computer will also contain any programs you have installed yourself. You can find more information on setting up new programs in Lesson 12.

STARTING A PROGRAM

Windows uses folders to keep your programs organized. Rather than have one long list of programs, you can organize the programs into groups, each in its own folder. To start a program, you open the folder and click the program icon. Follow these steps:

1. Click the Start menu and select Programs. You see a list of the program folders and icons on your system (see Figure 10.1).

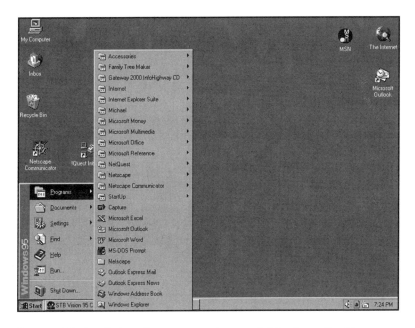

FIGURE 10.1 Select the program icon or folder from the Programs menu.

2. If you see the program icon, click it to start the program.

   If the program is stored in a folder, point to the folder. Do this until you see the program icon. Then click the icon to start the program.

Most of your time spent using Windows is spent using some type of application; therefore, you might want to investigate some alternative methods for starting programs. The next section covers some shortcuts you can try.

Shortcuts for Starting a Program

The Start menu isn't the only method for starting a program. Windows 95 provides several other methods, as covered here.

Starting a Program with a Shortcut Icon

For programs you use all the time, you may want to put a shortcut to that program right on the desktop. Then you can simply double-click the shortcut icon to start the program. You can learn how to create shortcut icons in Lesson 16.

Starting a Program and Opening a Document

If you want to both open a document and start a program, you can use the Documents command. Windows 95 keeps track of the last 15 documents you worked on. You can open any of these documents (and at the same time start that program) by following these steps:

1. Click the Start button.

2. Select the Documents command. You see a list of documents you have recently worked on (see Figure 10.2).

3. Click the document you want to open. Windows starts the program and opens the document you selected.

You can then continue working on this document. Remember to save your changes!

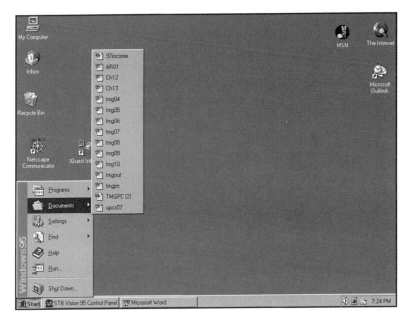

FIGURE 10.2   Select any of the last 15 documents you have worked on.

USING THE RUN COMMAND

You can also use the Run command to start a program. To use this command, you need to know the name of the program as well as the path of folders where this program is stored. Usually Run is used to install new programs. Follow these steps to use the Run command:

1. Click the Start button.

2. Select the Run command. You see the Run dialog box (see Figure 10.3).

3. In the Open text box, type the program name. Be sure to include the complete path to the program.

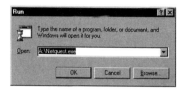

FIGURE 10.3   Type the program name to run the program.

  Take Your Time and Browse   If you aren't sure where the program is stored, you can use the Browse button to browse through the folders on your system, finding the file you want.

4. Click the OK button.

The program is started. For instance, if you use the Run command to start an installation program, you see that installation program. Follow the on-screen prompts to install the program.

STARTING A PROGRAM EACH TIME YOU START WINDOWS

As a final method, you can also put programs in your Startup folder. Each time you start Windows, all programs in this folder are started. For more information on this topic, see Lesson 16.

In this lesson, you learned how to start a program. For more information on key program skills, read the next lesson.

LEARNING
BASIC
PROGRAM
SKILLS

In this lesson, you learn some skills that you will use over and over in programs, including selecting text, saving a document, and printing.

SELECTING TEXT

While this book can't tell you how to use each of the applications you have on your PC, it can teach you some key skills used in many programs. Probably the most common skill is selecting something (text, numbers, an object). When you want to work with something, you start by selecting it. If you want to make text bold, you select the text. If you want to chart a set of figures, you select the data to chart. If you want to copy an object you've drawn, you select that object. Selecting is the first step for many editing and formatting tasks.

To select text, follow these steps:

1. Click at the start of the text you want to select.

2. Hold down the mouse button and drag across the text.

3. Release the mouse button. The text appears in reverse video as shown in Figure 11.1.

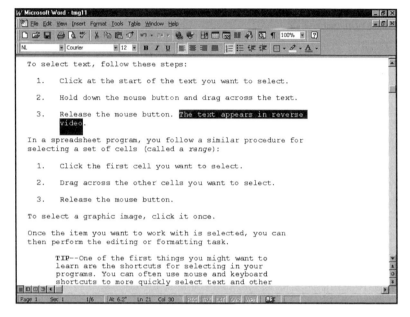

FIGURE 11.1 Select text by dragging the mouse across it.

In a spreadsheet program, you follow a similar procedure for selecting a set of cells (called a *range*):

1. Click the first cell you want to select.
2. Drag across the other cells you want to select.
3. Release the mouse button.

To select a graphic image, click it once.

Once the item you want to work with is selected, you can then perform the editing or formatting task.

Learn the Shortcuts One of the first things you might want to learn are the shortcuts for selecting in your programs. You can often use mouse and keyboard shortcuts to more quickly select text and other data.

COPYING, CUTTING, AND PASTING TEXT

One of the greatest benefits of an electronic document is that the data is not yet committed to paper; therefore, you can easily make editing changes. You can delete text you don't need, move text to a different location, or copy text you want to reuse.

Windows programs use the metaphor of scissors and paste for these editing tasks. You first "cut" the text you want to move or copy and then "paste" the text to its new location. If your program includes a toolbar, look for buttons for cutting, copying, and pasting. You can also find these commands in the Edit menu of most programs. The process for moving and copying text is similar from program to program.

DELETING TEXT

To delete text, follow these steps:

1. Select the text you want to delete.

2. Press the Delete key. The other text is adjusted to fill in the gap.

You can delete unwanted text. As another editing change, you may want to rearrange the text in a document. The next section covers how to move text.

MOVING TEXT

To move text, follow these steps:

1. Select the item you want to move. To select text or a range in a worksheet, drag across it. To select a graphic object, click it.

2. Click the Cut button, or open the Edit menu and select the Cut command.

3. Move the mouse to where you want to paste the text. Click once so that the cursor is in the correct place.

4. Click the Paste button, or open the Edit menu and select the Paste command.

The text is pasted to the new location. In addition to moving text, you can also copy text from one spot to another.

COPYING TEXT

Copying text is similar to moving, but you will have two copies of the selected text: one in the original spot and one where you paste the copy. Follow these steps:

1. Select the item you want to copy.

2. Click the Copy button, or open the Edit menu and select the Copy command.

3. Move the mouse to where you want to place the copy. Click once so that the cursor is in the correct place.

4. Click the Paste button, or open the Edit menu and select the Paste command.

Moving Between Documents   You can copy or move text to another document. To do so, simply move to that document after cutting or copying and then paste the selection into the new document.

The text is pasted to the new location. You now have two copies of the selected text.

SAVING A DOCUMENT

One of the most important things you can learn about using a PC is to save your work. There's nothing more frustrating than spending hours getting every word in a document just perfect and then having some accident happen before you've saved. If the power goes off, if your system crashes, if you turn off the PC without saving—all that work is lost. You should get in the habit of saving your work and saving often.

When you save a document, you do two things. First, you select a location for the file—a folder on your hard disk where the file will be stored. Second, you enter a name. You can enter up to 255 characters, including spaces for a name if you are using Windows 95. (Previous versions of Windows limited you to an 8-character name.) Use something descriptive, but don't go overboard.

Again, the procedure for saving a document is similar from application to application. The following steps use WordPad as an example. In your program, you may find other features and options for saving, but the general process is the same.

Follow these steps to save a document:

1. Open the <u>F</u>ile menu and select the <u>S</u>ave command. The first time you save the document you are prompted to select a location and file name (see Figure 11.2).

FIGURE 11.2   Enter a file name for the document you are saving.

2. Select a drive from the Save <u>in</u> drop-down list.

3. Select a folder from the folders listed. You can use the Up One Level button to move up one folder in the folder structure.

4. Type a file name.

5. Click the Save button.

Once you've saved the document once, you don't have to reenter the folder and file name. You can simply select File, Save to save the document to the same folder and with the same name.

 What Savings!   Look for a Save button in the toolbar as a shortcut for selecting the Save command. Also, to save a document with a new name or in a new location, use the File, Save As command.

OPENING A DOCUMENT

The purpose of saving a document is so that you can open it again. You may want to open a document so that you can use it again. Or perhaps you weren't finished: you need to make additional editing or formatting changes. When you want to work on a document you've saved previously, use the Open command by following these steps:

1. Open the File menu and select the Open command. You see the Open dialog box. Figure 11.3 shows the dialog box used for WordPad. The dialog box will look a little differently for other programs.

FIGURE 11.3   Use the Open dialog box to open documents you have previously saved.

2. If necessary, change to the drive and folder that contains
   the file. You can use the Look in drop-down list to select a
   different drive. Use the Up One Level button to move up
   a level in the folder structure.

3. When you see your file listed, double-click it.

 Open Sesame!   As a shortcut, look for an Open button
in the program toolbar.

PRINTING YOUR WORK

Most documents are created with the intent of being printed and
possibly distributed. If your printer is all connected and set up,
you can use the Print command to print. Follow these steps:

1. Open the File menu and select the Print command. Most
   programs display a Print dialog box where you can select
   such printing options as what to print and the number of
   copies to print (see Figure 11.4).

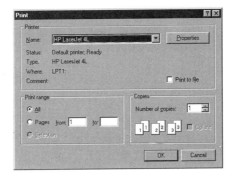

FIGURE 11.4   Use this dialog box to select options for printing a
document.

2. Make any changes to the options.

3. Click the OK button.

 Don't Miss the Previews   Many programs include a command for previewing a document. You can check the preview to see how the document flows on the page and then make any changes before printing. Look for a Print Preview button or a Print Preview command in the File menu.

In this lesson, you learned some key skills—selecting text; copying, moving, and deleting text; and saving, opening, and printing documents. The next lesson explains how to install new programs on your system.

INSTALLING A PROGRAM

In this lesson, you learn how to add new programs to your system.

PURCHASING A NEW PROGRAM

When you purchase a new PC, that system may come with some software programs. These programs might be enough to get you started, but as you use the PC more and more, you may find that you require other programs. (You can learn about the different program types in Lesson 3.) You may want to upgrade an existing program to the newest version, or you may want to purchase an entirely new program.

You can find software in some retail stores, in computer stores, and through mail order outlets. Scan through any computer magazine to get an idea of what programs are available as well as the cost. You can also use the Internet as a resource for researching and finding programs.

 Finders Keepers You can find freeware and shareware at many Internet sites. Freeware programs are provided free to you. Shareware programs are provided for you to try without cost. If you like the program, you can pay a small fee to register and continue using the program.

When you are looking for new programs to purchase, be sure that you can run that program on your system. Each program has system requirements—the type of microprocessor, amount of memory, hard disk space, video card, and any other required equipment. You can usually find these requirements printed on

the side of the software box. Check the requirements to be sure
your PC is capable of running the software.

Also, be sure that you get the right program for your system. If
you have Windows 95, get Windows 95 programs. You can also
purchase and run DOS and Windows 3.1 programs on Windows
95. If you have a Macintosh, get Macintosh programs. Most popular programs come in several versions.

As a final precaution, check to see how the software is distributed—on floppy disks or on a CD-ROM disc. If you have both a
floppy disk and a CD-ROM drive, you don't have to worry. But if
you don't have a CD-ROM drive, be sure to get the version on
floppy disks. CD-ROM discs have become the most popular
method for distributing programs, especially large programs.

INSTALLING A NEW PROGRAM

When you install a new program, the installation program will
copy the necessary program files from the disk(s) to your hard
disk and also set up program icon(s) for the program. You need to
specify which folder to use for the program files, where to place
the program icons in the Start menu, and what program options
you want to set. The options will vary depending on the program;
but you don't have to worry too much because the installation
program will guide you step-by-step through the process. You
simply have to get the installation program started.

You can use one of two methods to run the installation program.
You can use the Add/Remove Programs icon or the Run command. This section gives you the basic procedure for both. Be sure
to check the documentation that came with your software for
specific instructions.

USING THE ADD/REMOVE PROGRAMS ICON

Windows provides an Add/Remove Programs icon which you can
use to install new programs and remove (or uninstall programs).
Follow these steps:

1. Insert the installation disk in the drive.

Automation   If you are installing from a CD-ROM disc, that disc may have an AutoRun feature. If so, when you insert the disc, the installation program starts automatically.

2. Click the Start button, select Settings, and then select Control Panel. You see the program icons in the Control Panel.

3. Double-click the Add/Remove Programs icon.

4. If necessary, click the Install/Uninstall tab. You see the options for installing and uninstalling programs (see Figure 12.1).

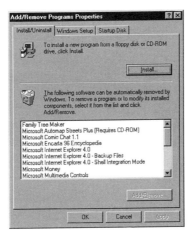

FIGURE 12.1   Use this dialog box to install new programs.

5. Click the Install button. Windows 95 looks on the floppy drive and CD-ROM disc for an installation program. It then displays the name of this program in the dialog box.

6. Click the Finish button to run this program. Windows 95 starts the program's installation program.

7. Follow the on-screen instructions for installing that particular program.

Try this method first; and if it doesn't work, then try using the Run command, covered next.

USING THE RUN COMMAND

You can also install a program by using the Run command to run the installation program. To use this method, you need to know the exact name of the program. It's usually named something like INSTALL.EXE or SETUP.EXE. Follow these steps to use the Run command:

1. Insert the program disk into the drive.

2. Click the Start button.

3. Select the Run command. The Run dialog box appears.

4. In the Open text box, type the program name. Remember to type the drive letter. Your floppy drive is usually Drive A. Your CD-ROM disc is usually Drive D (see Figure 12.2).

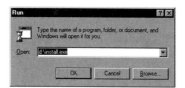

FIGURE 12.2   Type the installation program name.

Browse All You Want   If you aren't sure of the name of the installation program, type the drive name and then use Browse button to browse through the files on that drive. Select the installation file.

5. Click the OK button.

6. Follow the on-screen instructions for installing the program.

This section described how to install other programs. You can also add other Windows components using the Add/Remove Programs icon, as covered next.

INSTALLING WINDOWS ADDITIONAL COMPONENTS

When you install Windows 95, you have some options on which program components are installed. If you did not install Windows 95—or if you did and want to add other components (games, wallpaper, other program features)—you can do so using the Add/Remove Programs icon. Follow these steps:

1. Click the Start button, select Settings, and then select Control Panel. You see the program icons in the Control Panel.

2. Double-click the Add/Remove Programs icon.

3. Click the Windows Setup tab. You see the Windows components (see Figure 12.3). Items in the Components list that are checked are installed. Items that are blank are not installed. If there's a gray background and a check, only some of the items in that set are installed.

4. Check the components you want to install. Some components, like Accessories, are more than one component. To view the available options, select the component and then click the Details button. Check which components you want to install and then click the OK button.

5. Click the OK button.

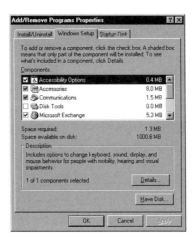

FIGURE 12.3 Use this dialog box to install other Windows components.

6. When prompted, insert the Windows 95 disks or CD-ROM disc. The necessary program files are copied to your Windows folder, and this component is added.

You can also uninstall programs with the Add/Remove Programs icon, and that's the topic of the next section.

UNINSTALLING A PROGRAM

If you have a program you no longer need, or if you upgrade a program and want to get rid of the previous version, you can uninstall it. You could simply delete the program folder; but keep in mind that the original program installation may have put files in other folders and also changed some system settings. The best way is to uninstall the program using the Add/Remove Program icon. Follow these steps:

1. Click the Start button, select Settings, and then select Control Panel. You see the program icons in the Control Panel.

2. Double-click the Add/Remove Programs icon.

3. If necessary, click the Install/Uninstall tab. You see the options for installing and uninstalling programs (refer to Figure 12.1).

4. Select the program you want to uninstall.

 It's Not Listed!   If the program is not listed in this dialog box, you cannot use this method. Check the program documentation for information on uninstalling the program.

5. Click the Add/Remove button. Windows 95 removes the program files and any shortcuts to the program.

In this lesson, you learned how to install and uninstall programs. The next lesson covers how to organize the files and folders on your hard disk.

13 LESSON

ORGANIZING YOUR FILES

In this lesson, you learn how to organize the files on your PC.

UNDERSTANDING FILES AND FOLDERS

The end result of most applications is some type of file—a memo, a sales report, a client list, a presentation, a newsletter. As you use your PC more and more, these files will multiply, so you need to think of how to organize the files.

The most common analogy used to describe files, folders, and hard disks is that of a filing cabinet. You can think of your hard disk as one big filing cabinet. If all your files were lumped together on the hard disk, finding the file you needed would be difficult, if not impossible. Instead, much like a filing cabinet has file folders, a hard disk can be divided into folders. You can then store like files together in a folder. A folder can contain files or other folders.

The folders you have on your system will vary. Usually programs are installed in their own folder, so you probably have a folder for each program on your system. That folder may contain other folders for different parts of the program. Windows 95, for instance, has its own folder with many subfolders for different items.

In addition to the folders already set up on your system, you can create your own folders, as covered later in this lesson.

Each time you create a document and save it, you are creating a file. (You learned about saving a file in Lesson 11.) That file is saved with a name in a particular location or folder on your hard drive. Here's a typical file name:

C:\My Documents\Using PCs\Chapter 1

This file name includes the drive (C), the path name or chain of folders where the file is stored (My Documents\Using PCs), and then finally the name assigned to the file (Chapter 1).

VIEWING YOUR SYSTEM CONTENTS

Windows 95 includes two tools for viewing and working with the folders and files on your system: My Computer and Windows Explorer.

USING MY COMPUTER

You can use My Computer to browse through the drives and folders on your system. The contents of each drive or folder are displayed in a separate window. Most novices prefer this method. Follow these steps:

1. Double-click the My Computer icon on your desktop.

2. Double-click the drive you want to open.

3. Double-click the folder you want to open.

4. Continue double-clicking folders until you find the folder or file you want to work with. Figure 13.1 shows an open folder with several data files.

5. To close a window, click the Close button.

If you prefer to use another method, you can use Windows Explorer.

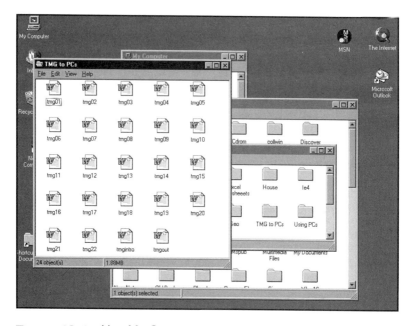

FIGURE 13.1   Use My Computer to browse through the folders on your system.

USING WINDOWS EXPLORER

You can also use Windows Explorer; this program presents your system in a hierarchical structure in a two-column window. Because you can see the entire system in one window, more advanced users may prefer this method. You can try both and see which you prefer. Follow these steps to start Windows Explorer:

1. Click the Start button.

2. Select Programs and then Windows Explorer. The program is started, and you see the contents of your system in a hierarchical view (see Figure 13.2).

3. To expand a folder (see the subfolders within), click the plus sign (+) next to the folder. To collapse the folder and hide these subfolders, click the minus (–) sign.

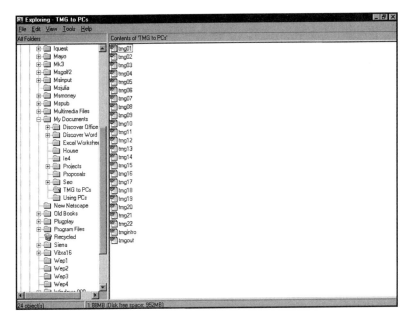

FIGURE 13.2   Use Windows Explorer for an overall view of all the drives on your system.

4. To view the contents of a drive or folder, click the item on the left side. The right side shows the contents of that selected item.

You can do lots of file management tasks with either My Computer or Windows Explorer. For instance, you can set up new folders. This topic is covered next.

CREATING NEW FOLDERS

As mentioned, to keep your files organized, you should create your own set of folders for your data files. The organization and names for your folders are up to you. You might want to use the My Documents folder and set up subfolders for different program types (Word documents, Excel worksheets, and so on). Or you might set up folders for each project. You can select whatever method you prefer.

To create a new folder, follow these steps:

1. To use My Computer, open the drive or folder where you want to place the new folder.

   To use Windows Explorer, select the drive or folder where you want to place the new folder.

2. Open the File menu and select the New command. In the submenu that appears, select Folder. Windows adds a new folder (named New Folder) to the window (see Figure 13.3). The name is highlighted so that you can type a more descriptive name.

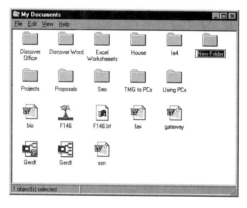

FIGURE 13.3 You can create new folders.

3. Type a name for the new folder and press Enter.

Once you create folders, you can use the other Windows features to work with them, as covered in the next section.

WORKING WITH FOLDERS

As mentioned, you can use either My Computer or Windows Explorer to display the contents of a particular folder. You can, for instance, open a folder and then make a backup copy of the files in that folder. (More on file stuff in the next lesson.) You can also delete, rename, copy, and move folders:

- To delete a folder, right-click the folder using either My Computer or Windows Explorer (see Figure 13.4). Select the Delete command and then click the Yes button to confirm the deletion. The folder and all of its contents are deleted.

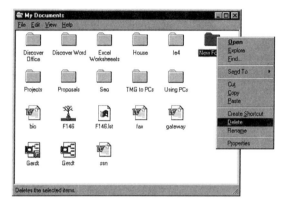

FIGURE 13.4   You can use the shortcut menu to work with folders on your system.

- To rename a folder, right-click the folder, select Rename, type a new name, and press Enter.

- To copy or move a folder, use Windows Explorer. This window displays your entire system in one window so that you can easily drag from one folder to another. To move, select the folder and then drag it to the new folder where you want it placed. To copy, hold down the Ctrl key and then drag to the new folder.

In this lesson, you learned how to work with the folders on your system. The next lesson covers how to handle the files on your PC.

MANAGING YOUR FILES

In this lesson, you learn how to take care of the data files you create when you use a computer.

DISPLAYING FILES

The first step in working with files is to display the file or files you want to work with. You can use either My Computer or Windows Explorer to display files.

USING MY COMPUTER

To use My Computer to view files, follow these steps:

1. Double-click the My Computer icon.

2. Double-click the drive you want to open.

3. Double-click the folder you want to open. Each time you double-click, a new window is opened, and that window displays the contents of the selected folder.

4. Continue opening folders until you see the files you want to work with.

If you want to try a different view for working with files, you can use Windows Explorer, covered in the next section.

USING WINDOWS EXPLORER

To use Windows Explorer to view files, follow these steps:

1. Click the Start button. Select Programs and then Windows Explorer. The program is started, and you see the contents of your system in a hierarchical view.

2. If necessary, expand the folder listing until you see the folder you want to open. To expand a folder (see the subfolders within), click the plus sign (+) next to the folder.

3. Click the folder you want to view on the left side. Windows Explorer displays the contents of the selected item on the right side.

Once you display the files, you can then work with them—copy, rename, delete, and so on. The first step for working with a file or group of files is to select the file(s) you want.

SELECTING FILES

For some tasks, you may want to work with a single file. To select a single file, click it. For other tasks, you may want to work with several files. For instance, you may want to back up all the files in a folder. To select multiple files, you can do any of the following:

- To select all files in a folder, open the Edit menu and select Select All.

- To select files next to each other, click the first file. Then hold down the Shift key and click the last file. All files in between the two are selected.

- To select files that are not next to each other, press and hold down the Ctrl key and then click each file you want to select. Figure 14.1 shows several files selected.

Once the file is selected, you can then carry out the task—delete the files, copy the files, and so on. The rest of this lesson covers these tasks.

FIGURE 14.1 You can select a single file or multiple files.

MOVING FILES

When keeping your files organized, you may need to move a file or files from one location to another. You may decide to use a different organization. Or maybe you inadvertently saved a document in the wrong folder, or perhaps your projects have grown so much you need to reorganize your files and put them in different folders.

The easiest way to move files is to use Windows Explorer. This program works better than My Computer because you can drag and drop the file all in one window.

To move a file or group of files from one folder to another, follow these steps:

1. Start Windows Explorer.

2. In the right pane, display the files you want to move.

3. Scroll the left pane until you see the folder to which you want to move the file(s).

4. Select the file(s) you want to move (see Figure 14.2).

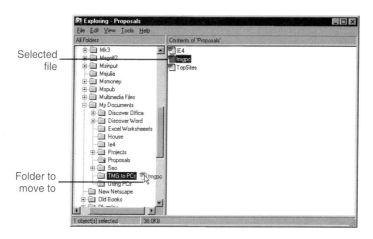

Selected file

Folder to move to

FIGURE 14.2   You can drag and drop files from one folder to another using Windows Explorer.

5. Hold down the mouse button and drag the files to the new folder in the left pane of the window. The files are moved.

Moving files deletes the selected files from one folder or drive and then copies them to another folder or drive. In some cases, you may want to have two copies of the files. That is, leave the files in the original location and copy them to another drive or folder.

COPYING FILES

Copying is similar to moving, but instead of one version of the selected file, you end up with two. For instance, you might need to copy all the files in a folder so that you have extra copies in case something happens to the originals. You might want to copy a file to a floppy disk so that you can take the file with you.

To copy from one folder to another, use Windows Explorer. To copy from your hard disk to a floppy disk, you can use either My Computer or Windows Explorer.

COPYING FROM FOLDER TO FOLDER

To copy from one folder to another using Windows Explorer, follow these steps:

1. Start Windows Explorer.

2. Display the files you want to copy on the right side of the window. Select these files.

3. On the left side, scroll through the window until you can see the drive or folder in which you want to place the copies.

4. Hold down the Ctrl key and drag the selected file(s) to the drive or folder where you want to place the copy.

The files are copied to the selected drive or folder.

COPYING FROM YOUR HARD DISK TO A FLOPPY DISK

The easiest way to copy from your hard disk to a floppy disk is to use the Send To command. Follow these steps:

1. Insert the floppy disk into the drive.

2. Display the files you want to copy using either My Computer or Windows Explorer.

3. Select the file(s) you want to copy.

4. Right-click the file(s).

5. From the shortcut menu, select Send To and then select your floppy drive (usually Drive A).

The files are copied to the floppy drive.

DELETING FILES

As you use your computer more and more, the files you have will multiply and eventually you will have to weed out the old, unneeded stuff. Deleting files you don't need frees up the disk space for new files.

When you delete a file or folder, keep in mind that Windows 95 does not really delete the file, but simply moves it to the Recycle Bin. You can undo the deletion and recover the item from the Recycle Bin if you make a mistake and delete a file you need. If you want to permanently get rid of the file, empty the Recycle Bin. This section covers all these tasks.

DELETING A FILE

Follow these steps to delete a file or group of files:

1. Using either My Computer or Windows Explorer, select the file(s) you want to delete.

2. Right-click the selected item(s) and then select the Delete command.

3. When prompted to confirm the deletion, click the Yes button.

The file is deleted. If you make a mistake, you can undo the deletion.

UNDELETING A FILE

To retrieve a file from the Recycle Bin, follow these steps:

1. On the desktop, double-click the Recycle Bin. You see the contents of this system folder (see Figure 14.3).

2. Select the items you want to undelete.

3. Right-click the selected items and then select the Restore command.

The item is returned to its original folder.

FIGURE 14.3 You can retrieve deleted items from the Recycle Bin.

EMPTYING THE RECYCLE BIN

As mentioned previously, files and folders aren't really deleted with the Delete command, but simply moved to the Recycle Bin, a temporary holding spot. To free up the disk space and really get rid of the file, you must empty the Recycle Bin. Follow these steps:

1. Double-click the Recycle Bin icon.

2. Check out the contents and be sure it does not contain any files or folders you want to keep. Once you empty the Recycle Bin, you can't get the contents back.

3. Open the File menu and select the Empty Recycle Bin command.

4. Confirm the deletion by clicking the Yes button.

All of the files and folders in the Recycle Bin are permanently deleted.

RENAMING FILES

When you save a file, you assign a name. If this name doesn't work—for instance, the file name isn't easy to remember—you can make a change. You can use up to 255 characters, including spaces. You cannot use any of the following characters:

\ ? : * " < > |

Shortening In some DOS and Windows applications, the folder name is truncated to the old 8-character limitation. When a program truncates a folder or file name, it adds a tilde (~) to indicate that the name has been shortened.

Follow these steps to rename a file:

1. In Windows Explorer or My Computer, display the file you want to rename.

2. Right-click the file and select Rename from the shortcut menu that appears. Windows highlights the current name and displays a box around it.

3. Type the new name and press Enter.

More Shortcuts For files or folders that you use all the time, consider creating a shortcut icon for the file or folder. You can find information on adding shortcuts to the desktop in Lesson 16.

In this lesson, you learned how to work with the files on your PC. The next lesson brings up a new topic—multimedia on the PC.

15

MULTIMEDIA ON THE PC

In this lesson, you learn how to take advantage of the multimedia capabilities of your PC.

WHAT IS MULTIMEDIA?

Multimedia is the combination of different medium—sound, video, text, graphics, animation, and so on. A multimedia document is a much richer presentation than just plain old text. You can find multimedia presentations, documents, programs, and Web pages. For example, you might have a multimedia encyclopedia. When you look up an entry for Beethoven, you can not only read a text account of his life and accomplishments, but also play a sample of one of his symphonies. The entry might also include a picture of the famous composer.

Multimedia presentations are becoming more and more prevalent. These types of presentations are being used not only in encyclopedias and other reference tools, but also for selling a product or teaching a new concept.

To take advantage of these multimedia programs, you basically need a CD-ROM drive, sound card, and speakers. As multimedia presentations and programs became more popular, the equipment to run these features became standard equipment on a PC. If you have a new PC, you probably have a PC with this equipment. If you don't, you can purchase a multimedia upgrade package to add this equipment.

With the right hardware, you can run any of the multimedia software like games, encyclopedias, and so on. You can also use some of the Windows 95 applications to try out multimedia features, as covered in this lesson.

Playing Music

If you like music, you can use CD Player (included with Windows 95) to play your audio CDs. Keep in mind that the sound quality isn't going to be as great as if you were playing the CDs on your CD player. Even though most sound cards come with speakers that are adequate for playing sounds, don't expect excellent quality.

Playing a CD

To play a CD, follow these steps:

1. Click the Start button, select Programs, select Accessories, select Multimedia, and (finally) select CD Player. Windows starts the CD Player program (see Figure 15.1).

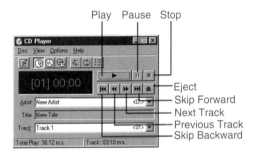

Figure 15.1   Use this program to play CDs.

2. Insert a disc into your CD drive and click the Play button. CD Player plays the first track on the CD. You can see the current track number and amount of time the CD has been playing in the CD Player window.

 You can minimize the CD Player window, and the CD will continue to play.

To play a different track, follow these steps:

1. In the CD Player window, display the Track drop-down list.

2. Click the track you want to play.

USING THE CD PLAYER TOOLBAR

The CD Player gives you a lot of information about what is playing currently, the current track number, and how much time has passed. At the bottom of the window, the CD Player displays the total play time and the time the current track has played.

In addition, the CD Player includes buttons that enable you to start a song over, switch to a different song, stop a song, and so on. Refer to Figure 15.1 to see the buttons in the CD drive Player window (see Table 15.1).

TABLE 15.1   CD PLAYER BUTTONS

NAME	DESCRIPTION
Play	Starts playing the CD.
Pause	Pauses the CD. To resume play, click the Play button again.
Stop	Stops the CD.
Previous Track	Plays the previous track.
Next Track	Plays the next track.
Skip Forward	Moves forward within the current track.
Skip Backward	Moves backward within the current track.
Eject	Ejects the CD.

PLAYING SOUNDS

Not only can you play audio CDs on your computer, you also can play other sounds. And you can record your own sounds with Sound Recorder, another Windows 95 program.

 Sounding Off   You can assign a sound to a Windows event so that when that event occurs (when an alert dialog box appears, for example), you hear a sound. For information on reviewing these sounds and making any changes, see Lesson 16.

You can play back most sounds without a sound card; Sound Recorder can use the computer's speaker. The sound will play better, though, if you have a sound card.

PLAYING A SOUND

Sounds, like all information on a computer, are stored in files. Most sound files are WAV files. You can play back sounds that you have recorded, or sounds provided with some other application. You also can download sounds from bulletin board systems or purchase sound files.

To play a sound, follow these steps:

1. Click the Start button, select Programs, select Accessories, select Multimedia, and select Sound Recorder. Windows displays the Sound Recorder window.

2. Open the File menu and select Open. In the Open dialog box that appears, change to the drive and folder that contains the file. Windows includes some sample sound files in the WINDOWS\MEDIA folder.

3. When you see the sound file you want to play, double-click it. In the Sound Recorder window, the name of the sound appears in the title bar (see Figure 15.2).

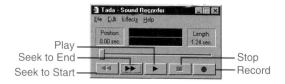

FIGURE 15.2   Use Sound Recorder to play back sounds.

4. To play the sound, click the Play button. Sound Recorder plays the sound. As it plays, you see the sound wave in the Sound Recorder window.

USING THE SOUND RECORDER TOOLBAR

You can use the buttons in the Sound Recorder window to play, rewind, or fast forward the sound. Figure 15.2 identifies the buttons for playing and recording sounds (see Table 15.2).

TABLE 15.2   SOUND RECORDER BUTTONS

NAME	DESCRIPTION
Seek To Start	Rewinds to the beginning of the sound file.
Seek To End	Fast forwards to the end of the sound file.
Play	Plays the sound.
Stop	Stops the playback.
Record	Records a new sound.

RECORDING SOUNDS

To record sounds, you need a sound card and a microphone, and the microphone must be plugged into your sound card. Most sound cards come with a microphone, but it may not have been connected. Check your sound card manual for help on where to plug in the microphone.

Follow these steps to record a sound:

1. In the Sound Recorder window, open the File menu and select New.

2. Click the Record button to start recording.

3. Speak into the microphone to record your sound. You see a visual representation of the sound wave as you make your recording.

 Short and Sweet Because sound files can be really huge, you should try to keep your message short and concise.

4. When you finish recording, click the Stop button. You can play back the sound by clicking the Play button.

5. To save the sound, open the File menu and select Save. The Save As dialog box appears.

6. In the Save As dialog box, change to the drive and folder where you want to store the file. Then type a file name in the File name text box and click the Save button.

PLAYING MEDIA CLIPS AND MOVIES

If you have multimedia presentations, you can use the Windows 95 Media Player to play them back. (Windows includes some sample files in the WINDOWS\MEDIA folder.) You can play back the following types of files:

- Video for Windows (AVI files)

- Sound (WAV files)

- MIDI music files (MID and RMI)

Many Internet sites also include movies that you can play back.

PLAYING A MEDIA FILE

Follow these steps to play a media file:

1. Click the Start button, select Programs, select Accessories, select Multimedia, and select Media Player. Windows displays the Media Player program.

2. Open the File menu and select Open. The Open dialog box appears with the Media folder selected. You can open files in this folder. Or if necessary, change to the appropriate drive and folder.

3. When you see the file you want to play, double-click it. You see the Media Player window with the name of the file in the title bar (see Figure 15.3).

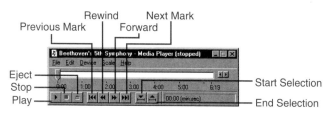

FIGURE 15.3   You can play back media files using Media Player.

4. To play the clip, click the Play button. Media Player plays back the media clip.

USING THE MEDIA PLAYER TOOLBAR BUTTONS

The buttons in the Media Player window enable you to play, rewind, and stop the playback. Table 15.3 identifies each button.

TABLE 15.3   MEDIA PLAYER BUTTONS

NAME	DESCRIPTION
Play	Plays the file.
Pause	Pauses the file.

NAME	DESCRIPTION
Stop	Stops playing the file.
Eject	Ejects a disc (if you are playing a file from a disc).
Previous Mark	Moves to the previous mark (if you have marked a selection of the file to play using the Start and End Selection buttons).
Rewind	Rewinds the file.
Fast Forward	Fast forward through the file.
Next Mark	Moves to the next marked section (if you have marked a selection or portion of the file to play).
Start Selection	Specifies the starting point (so you that can play part of a file).
End Selection	Tells Media Player where to end a selection (when you play part of a file).

In this lesson, you learned how to try some of the multimedia features of Windows 95. The next lesson explains how to make some customization changes to Windows.

16

CUSTOMIZING YOUR PC

In this lesson, you learn how to customize Windows 95.

CHANGING THE DESKTOP

The desktop is the background of the Windows 95 screen. If you don't like the plain background, you can make some changes. You can use wallpaper, use a pattern, change the color scheme, and use a screensaver, as covered in this section.

USING WALLPAPER OR A PATTERN

Windows comes with several wallpaper and pattern designs (BMP files) that it installs in the \WINDOWS folder. You can select from several different wallpaper and patterns including argyle, cars, bricks, pinstripe, or zigzag.

 Decisions, Decisions You can select a pattern or wallpaper, but not both. If you select both, the wallpaper takes precedence.

Follow these steps to select a wallpaper or pattern for the desktop:

1. Right-click the desktop and select Properties from the shortcut menu that appears. The Display Properties dialog box appears, with the Background tab selected.

2. In the Wallpaper list, select the wallpaper you want to use.

   Or, in the Pattern list, select the pattern you want. Figure 16.1 shows a preview of a selected pattern.

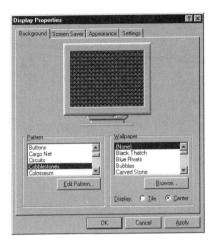

FIGURE 16.1 Select a wallpaper or pattern for your desktop from this dialog box.

3. Click the OK button.

Changing the desktop to a pattern or wallpaper is just one change you can make. You can also change the colors used.

USING A DIFFERENT COLOR SCHEME

With Windows 95, you can customize the colors used for on-screen elements, including the active title bar, the desktop, the application background, or the menus. The easiest way is to use one of the predefined color schemes. To do so, follow these steps:

1. Right-click the desktop and select Properties from the shortcut menu. The Display Properties dialog box appears.

2. Click the Appearance tab.

3. Display the Scheme drop-down list box and select the color scheme you want to use. You see a preview of how the desktop will look using this new scheme (see Figure 16.2).

FIGURE 16.2   Select a different color scheme for your desktop using the options in this dialog box.

4. Click the OK button. Windows uses the selected scheme for all on-screen elements.

The Display Properties dialog box also includes a tab for adding a screen saver. This is the topic of the next section.

USING A SCREEN SAVER

If you left an image on-screen for a long time on older PC monitors, that image could become burned in. (You can sometimes see a burned-in image on ATM machines.) To prevent burn-in, someone came up with the idea of a screen saver. If you didn't use your computer for a certain period of time, the computer would automatically display an animated graphic, which would prevent burn-in.

Today's monitors don't have burn-in problems, but some users still use a screen saver, mostly for show. If you don't use your PC for a certain amount of time, Windows displays a moving graphic image. Windows 95 includes several screen savers you can try.

Make It Stop   To stop the screen saver and return to your program, press any key or move the mouse.

Follow these steps to use a screen saver:

1. Right-click the desktop and select Properties from the shortcut menu. The Display Properties dialog box appears.

2. Click the Screen Saver tab.

3. Display the Screen Saver drop-down list and select the screen saver you want. To see a preview, click the Preview button. Figure 16.3 shows a preview of a screen saver.

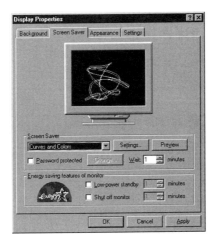

FIGURE 16.3   You can use a screen saver for your monitor.

4. In the Wait text box, enter the number of minutes you want Windows to wait before displaying the image.

5. Click the OK button.

The desktop also includes the taskbar, and you can make some changes to this on-screen element. See the next section for information on this customizing change.

CHANGING THE TASKBAR

The taskbar is within easy reach right at the bottom of your screen. If you don't want it displayed or if you want to move it to a different location, you can do so. You can also change how the taskbar appears.

MOVING THE TASKBAR

To move the taskbar, follow these steps:

1. Click a blank area of the taskbar and hold down the mouse button.

2. Drag the taskbar to another edge of the screen.

When you release the mouse button, the taskbar appears in the new location. You can also resize the taskbar.

RESIZING THE TASKBAR

To resize the taskbar, follow these steps:

1. Position the mouse pointer on the taskbar edge that borders the desktop. The pointer becomes a two-headed arrow.

2. Drag the border to the size you want.

The taskbar is resized. You can also make some other changes to how the taskbar appears.

SELECTING TASKBAR OPTIONS

Follow these steps to set taskbar options:

1. Open the Start menu, select Settings, and select Taskbar.

2. Make any changes to the following options:

   Check the Always On Top option to have the taskbar always appear on top of any other window on the screen.

Check the Auto Hide option to have Windows hide the taskbar from view. You can make the taskbar pop up by moving the mouse pointer to the bottom edge of the screen.

Check Show Small Icons in the Start menu to use smaller icons for items in the Start menu.

Check Show Clock to display the clock; uncheck this option to turn off the clock.

3. Click the OK button.

Another desktop change is to create shortcut icons to your favorite programs, files, or folders.

CREATING SHORTCUTS

In your work, you may find there's one program, folder, or file you use all the time. For quick access to a program, file, or folder, you can create a shortcut to it and place the shortcut on the desktop. Double-click a folder shortcut, and you see the contents of that folder. Double-click a file shortcut, and that file is opened. Double-click a program shortcut, and the program is started.

Follow these steps to create a shortcut:

1. In Windows Explorer or My Computer, select the program, file, or folder for which you want to create a shortcut. Be sure that you can see at least part of the desktop.

2. With the right mouse button, drag the icon from the window to the desktop.

3. From the shortcut menu, select Create Shortcut(s) Here. Windows adds the shortcut to the desktop.

 What's in a Name?   To rename the shortcut icon, right-click the icon, select the Rename command, type a new name, and press Enter.

The shortcut is not the actual file, but a pointer to it. You can delete the shortcut by right-clicking it and selecting Delete. The original program, file, or folder is not affected.

ADDING SOUNDS TO EVENTS

You may have noticed that when you make a mistake or click somewhere you shouldn't, you hear a sound. You may also hear sounds for other events. That's because you can have Windows play a sound when a certain event happens. You can review the associated sounds and make any changes by following these steps:

1. Open the Start menu, select Settings, and select Control Panel.

2. Double-click the Sounds icon. Windows 95 displays the Sounds Properties dialog box (see Figure 16.4). Events that already have sounds attached to them are marked with a speaker icon.

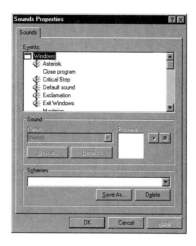

FIGURE 16.4   Use this dialog box to attach sounds to key Windows events.

3. To play a sound associated with an event, click the event and then click the Play button.

4. To attach a sound to an event or to change the sound
    currently attached to an event, click the event in the
    Events list. Then select a sound file from the Name list.

5. Click the OK button when you're finished.

 Customization   You can use other Control Panel programs to customize other options such as the mouse,
keyboard, and regional settings. You can experiment by
double-clicking the icon in the Control Panel folder and
reviewing the different options.

In this lesson, you learned how to make some customization
changes to Windows 95. The next lesson explains how to take
care of your PC.

17 TAKING CARE OF YOUR PC

In this lesson, you learn how to perform some maintenance tasks for your PC.

TAKING CARE OF DATA FILES

If something happens to your programs, you can always reinstall them; but if something happens to your data files, and you don't have a backup copy, you are stuck. Your data is invaluable; therefore, you should come up with a solid strategy for ensuring its safety.

You should periodically back up all the files on your PC. This type of backup is called a full backup. In addition to these complete backup sets, you may want to set a daily, weekly, or monthly backup plan for the files that have been changed. How often you should back up depends on how critical the data is to you and your business. If you get daily orders in your business, for instance, you may want to back up daily. If you use your PC a few times a week to create documents, you may want to back up once a week or once a month.

Backing up essentially copies all the files on your system in a compressed format to another drive. You can back up to floppy disks, to another hard drive, or to a special tape backup drive. You can use the backup program included with Windows 95 or purchase a separate backup program. If your backup is critical to your business, you may want to purchase a tape backup unit which speeds the backup process.

Safe Haven Be sure to put your backup copies in a safe place away from your computer. In case of some type of catastrophe (fire or theft, for example), you will want your backup copies in a secure location.

To run the Windows 95 backup program, follow these steps:

1. Double-click the My Computer icon.

2. Right-click the disk you want to back up, and then select Properties from the shortcut menu that appears.

3. In the drive Properties dialog box, click the Tools tab.

4. Click the Backup Now button. Follow the instructions for backing up. For complete information on all backup features, consult the online help for the backup program.

In addition to taking care of your data files, you should also consider how to maintain your program files, as covered next.

TAKING CARE OF PROGRAMS

Your programs are what you use day-to-day. You should follow a few strategies to keep your programs in tip-top shape:

- Store your program disks and manuals in a safe place. If something happens to the original program, you can always reinstall from these disks.

- Just because you can use the program disks more than once does not mean that you can share the program with someone else. Doing so is illegal.

- Consider registering your software with the software company. Doing so will make sure you know about any new versions (or fixes to problems in existing versions).

- Be sure to exit the program before you turn off the PC. Exiting when a program is still running can cause problems.

TAKING CARE OF YOUR HARD DISK

Your hard disk is like your treasure chest: it stores your programs and data files. In addition to backing up, you should periodically check the drive for errors. You may also want to improve performance by defragmenting the drive, as covered here.

CHECKING A DRIVE FOR ERRORS

Hard drives can develop problems. Sometimes files do not get stored in the appropriate "cubbyhole" or cluster. Sometimes file names don't match up with the folders in which they're stored. To check for and fix any errors, you can use ScanDisk, a program included with Windows 95. Follow these steps:

1. Double-click the My Computer icon to display the contents of your computer.

2. Right-click the disk you want to check.

3. Select Properties from the shortcut menu that appears.

4. Click the Tools tab. This tab includes programs you can use to manage and optimize your disk drives (see Figure 17.1).

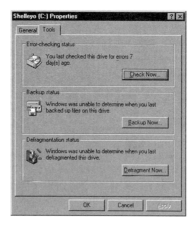

FIGURE 17.1   The Tools tab provides access to disk management tools like ScanDisk.

5. Click the Check Now button. Windows displays the ScanDisk dialog box.

6. Click the Start button to start checking the drive. Windows checks your drive. If it finds any errors, it displays a dialog box that explains the error and gives you options for repairing the error, deleting the file, or ignoring the error.

7. Select a correction method for each problem, and then click OK. When ScanDisk is complete, you see a summary of its findings.

8. Review this information and then click the Close button.

Another way to keep your hard disk in tip top shape is to defragment it, which is discussed in the next section.

IMPROVING HARD DISK PERFORMANCE BY DEFRAGMENTING

To understand why defragmenting can improve performance, you need to understand a little about how data is stored on your hard drive. Your hard disk is divided into little cubbyholes, called *clusters*. Clusters are further divided into *sectors*. All the clusters on one hard drive are the same size, but the size of clusters may vary from one hard drive to another.

When you save a file, Windows puts as much of the file as possible in the first cluster it finds. If the file won't fit into one cluster, Windows moves to the next available cluster and puts more of the file in it. This continues until Windows finds room for all the pieces of the file. The file allocation table, or FAT, keeps track of where the files are stored. When you open a file, Windows can go to the first cluster and get that part of the file, go to the second cluster and get that part of the file, and so on until it reads the entire file.

On a new drive, the clusters used to store the files are contiguous (next to each other), so you don't have much delay as Windows collects the different pieces of the files. As you use the drive more and add and delete files, the open clusters become scattered; and when you store a file, its pieces are scattered all over the drive. That is, the disk is *fragmented*, and you may find that it takes longer to open a file.

To improve the performance, you can straighten up the disk and put the files back in order by defragmenting the disk. Windows 95 includes Disk Defragmenter, a defragmentation program that reads the clusters on the drive and then rearranges them so that they are in a better order.

 Good Things   It's a good idea to back up your system before you make a major change such as defragmenting your hard disk.

Follow these steps to defragment your hard drive:

1. Double-click the My Computer icon.

2. Right-click the disk you want to check.

3. From the submenu that appears, select Properties.

4. In the drive Properties dialog box, click the Tools tab.

5. Click the Defragment Now button. Defrag analyzes the drive and displays the Disk Defragmenter dialog box. The Disk Defragmenter also makes a recommendation on whether defragmenting is needed (see Figure 17.2).

Figure 17.2   You can defragment your hard drive to improve performance.

6. Click the <u>S</u>tart button. Windows displays the progress of the defragmentation process on-screen.

 Details   To see a detailed map of the changes, click the Show Details button and then click the Legend button. You see a map of the clusters on the system as they are being read and written.

7. When the defragmentation is complete and you are prompted to defragment another drive, click the No button.

You know how to take care of your software and your data files. You should also pay attention to your hardware.

TAKING CARE OF YOUR HARDWARE

In addition to the intangible elements of your computer, you also need to take care of the physical components. Here are some tips to consider:

- If you drink or smoke next to the PC, be careful. Both can damage hardware elements.

- Don't spray cleaner directly on the monitor or any other PC part. Instead, spray a rag and then use the rag to clean the components.

- Be careful when moving the system unit. Don't drop, jar, or otherwise beat up on this sensitive piece of equipment.

- Don't ever attach new equipment to the PC when the computer is on. Always turn off the computer if you are making any connections.

- Use a surge protector to protect against power surges.

In this lesson, you learned how to take proper care of your PC. The next lesson brings up a new topic, the Internet.

18

USING THE INTERNET

In this lesson, you learn the basics about the Internet—what it is, what you can do, and what you need to get connected.

WHAT IS THE INTERNET?

You can barely pick up the paper or watch TV without some reference to the Internet. Your *grandmother* might even be hooked up to the Internet. What is the Internet and why is it so exciting?

The Internet is basically a network of networks. From your home PC, you can connect through the phone lines to one of these networks. From that network, you can hook up to another network, to another network, to another network. You can journey to sites in town, across town, in another city, in another state, in another country! All without leaving the comfort of your desk.

The wealth of information published on the Internet is overwhelming. You can find museums, shopping malls, financial news networks, sports columns and stats, software, music and entertainment news, medical labs, and more. There's no easy way to categorize the information on the Internet. Suffice to say that if there's something you want to find, you can probably find it somewhere on the Internet. That's what makes the Internet so exciting—there is literally something for everyone.

WHAT CAN YOU DO ON THE INTERNET?

Once connected to the Internet, you can do several different things:

- **View World Wide Web pages.** The World Wide Web is graphical sites that can contain not only text and graphics, but also sounds, movies, animations, programs, and other multimedia elements. The World Wide Web is a rich publishing environment. You learn more about "surfing" the Web in the next lesson.

- **Send e-mail messages.** If you know someone with an e-mail address, you can send that person a message, even attaching a file if needed. E-mail has become *the* way to stay connected to friends, family, and coworkers. Lesson 20 covers some basic e-mail tasks.

- **Participate in online discussions.** You can read messages posted on an electronic bulletin board and respond. This collection of bulletin boards is known as *newsgroups*. You learn more about newsgroups in Lesson 21.

- **Download files from a site to your PC.** You can download new versions of software programs, try demo programs, and review other text, sound, movie, and graphic files.

 FTP Sites that are set up for the transfer of files are called ftp (file transfer protocol) sites. The address to this type of site starts with **ftp:**.

WHAT DO YOU NEED TO ACCESS THE INTERNET?

If all this sounds exciting, you may be ready to sign up. To do so, you need a modem, phone line, Internet provider, and software.

 For More Information   If you want more information about getting connected to the Internet, try Que's *The Complete Idiot's Guide to the Internet.*

WHAT HARDWARE DO YOU NEED?

If your system already has a modem, you are set. If not, adding a modem is a fairly easy upgrade. In addition to the modem, you need a phone line. You can use an existing line, but then you need to coordinate when that line is a "phone" and when the line is an Internet connection. Instead, you may want to add a separate phone line for your modem.

WHAT IS AN INTERNET PROVIDER?

You also need an Internet service provider (ISP). This company provides you with a hookup to their network. From their network, you can get connected to the Internet. The ISP also provides the necessary programs to browse the Internet, handle e-mail, and read newsgroup messages (covered in the next lesson).

One easy way to get connected to the Internet is through an online service like America Online. You can take advantage of all the features of the online service in addition to using it as a gateway to the Internet. You can also find an independent service provider that focuses just on Internet connections. These may provide additional features, such as helping you publish your own Web page.

You can find independent service providers by looking in the Yellow Pages, by asking friends and coworkers for recommendations, or by checking out one of the many Internet directories or magazines for information.

Most providers charge a flat fee for unlimited usage, although this may vary from area to area and plan to plan. If they don't charge a flat fee, you may pay a certain amount for so much time. Over that time, you may be billed hourly. Check out the various plans offered by your provider.

 Comparison Shop Shop around for Internet service providers and compare what they have to offer. You can not only compare the price of the service, but also look into such things as technical support, the type of connections they provide, and so on.

WHAT SOFTWARE DO YOU NEED?

For each of the tasks you do on the Internet, you need a program for handling that particular task. For instance, to browse the World Wide Web, you need a Web browser. To read and send e-mail messages, you need an e-mail program. To participate in newsgroups, you need a newsreader.

Usually your ISP provides the necessary software. You can also use two popular programs, Netscape Communicator and Internet Explorer, to access the Internet. Both of these programs are really a complete suite of Internet tools and include all the programs you need to browse, send e-mail, transfer files, join newsgroups, and so on.

Netscape Navigator was one of the first and most successful Web browsers. It is now part of a suite of Internet tools called Netscape Communicator. Netscape's browser is offered free for a trial period. Then if you plan on using the browser, you need to pay a small fee. You can get more information about Netscape at **home.netscape.com**, Netscape's home page (see Figure 18.1).

(You learn more about Web pages and addresses in the next lesson.)

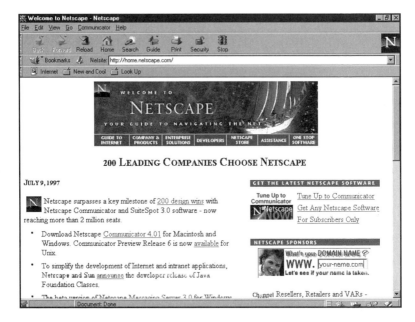

FIGURE 18.1   Netscape Communicator is a popular Web browser.

Microsoft entered the Internet market a little late, but its product—Internet Explorer—is comparable to Netscape Communicator. Internet Explorer is free, and you can download this browser at Microsoft's Web site (**home.microsoft.com**). Figure 18.2 shows Internet Explorer.

In this lesson, you learned what the Internet is. The next lesson describes some basic browsing.

FIGURE 18.2   You can browse the Internet using Microsoft's
Internet Explorer.

19

L E S S O N

BASIC INTERNET BROWSING

In this lesson, you learn some basic skills for browsing the Internet.

LOGGING ON TO THE INTERNET

To get connected to the Internet, you need an Internet account, either through an Internet service provider (ISP) or an online service. You also need to follow the instructions for installing the software for getting connected. Finally, your Internet service provider will give you specific instructions for how to log on to the Internet. Here are the basic steps:

1. Double-click the Internet icon. Usually the installation program sets up an icon for Internet access.

2. When prompted, sign on to your Internet provider. Usually you type your user name and password. Figure 19.1 shows the sign in for my Internet provider.

FIGURE 19.1 For most Internet connections, you type your user name and password.

When you connect, you see your home page, which will vary depending on which browser you are using.

UNDERSTANDING A WEB PAGE

Everything on the Web is displayed as a document page, and a Web page can contain text, graphics, sounds, movies, and links to other Web pages. These links are what make it possible to browse the Web. When you click a link, you're taken to another page on the Web, which contains information as well as other links. A link may take you to another page in that document, to another document at that site, or to an entirely new site. The journey is half the fun!

Links usually appear underlined; images also may be links. Figure 19.2 shows a typical Web page. Not only can you review the information and pictures on this page, but you can also click any of the links to get additional information.

FIGURE 19.2   A typical Web page includes text, graphics, and links to other Web pages.

Each Web page has a unique address called an URL, or uniform resource locator. For example, here's the address for the White House:

http://www.whitehouse.gov

You can use this address to go directly to the page, as covered in the next section.

SURFING THE WEB

To navigate around the Web, you can click the links until you find the page you want. Or, you can type the address to go directly to the page. More and more, you'll find Web addresses advertised on business cards and in TV and print ads.

Both Netscape Communicator and Internet Explorer include toolbar buttons for navigating. For instance, Internet Explorer includes buttons for going back a page, forward a page, to the home page, and so on (see Figure 19.3). You can also use menu commands and other features for navigating through the Internet.

USING THE LINKS

To navigate from page to page using a link, follow these steps:

1. From any Web page, click the link. Links are usually underlined and/or may appear in a different color. Icons and other graphic images may also be links or hot spots. That page is displayed.

2. Continue clicking links until you find the information you want.

You can browse from link to link as one method to explore what's on the Internet. You can also go directly to an address.

FIGURE 19.3 Use the toolbar buttons to move from page to page.

GOING DIRECTLY TO AN ADDRESS

If going from link to link is too time-consuming, you may prefer a more direct method. If you know the address of the page, you can go directly to that page. Follow these steps:

1. Click in the Address text box. The entire address should be highlighted.

2. Type the address you want to go to and press Enter. You see that page.

Going to the address is great when you know the address, but what if you don't even know what site you are looking for? What if you just want to find out if there's a site for a particular topic? In that case, you can search the Web.

SEARCHING FOR A TOPIC ON THE WEB

Browsing around the Internet is time-consuming (but fun). You never know where you'll end up. You might start out researching a legitimate project and end up checking out pictures of bulldogs on the bulldog page. When you have an idea of what you want to find and want to see what's available, you can search the Web.

To search the Web, you use a search engine, and there are many different search engines available. They all work basically the same: you type the word or phrase you want to find and click the Search button. The search engine then displays matches. (You also can fine-tune the search using different search options.)

The search tools differ in how they search, that is, where they look for matches for your words. That means the results will vary. Also, how the results are displayed varies. Some display a short description. Some include some indication of how well the listed site matches the criteria you entered. Some may provide reviews of sites. For some, you can select what is displayed in the results list.

Both Internet Explorer and Netscape Communicator include a Search button, with links to popular search engines including Yahoo!, Magellan, InfoSeek, Alta Vista, Lycos, and Excite. You can experiment to see which one you like best.

 Try Again   If you search for a topic with one and don't get the results you like, try another one.

When you perform a search, you see a list of possible matches, and each one of these are links to that particular page. To go to that page, click the link.

Follow these steps to search the Internet:

1. Click the Search button in your browser's toolbar. You see a list of the different search engines from which you can select. Figure 19.4 shows the page of Internet Explorer search engines.

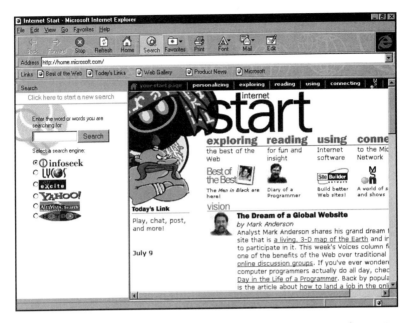

FIGURE 19.4   Select the search engine to use and enter the text to find.

2. Select the search engine you want to use.

3. In the text box, type the word or phrase you want to find and then click the Search button. You see the results of the search. Figure 19.5 shows the results of searching for tennis.

4. To go to any of the found sites, click the link to that site.

If additional sites were found, you can also display the next set of sites. Look for a link at the end of the list to display the next set of matches.

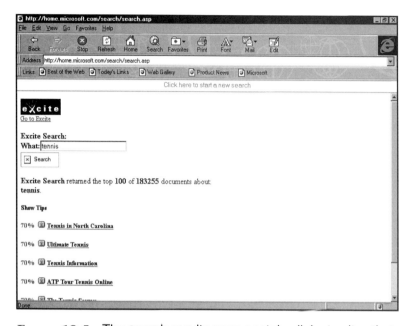

FIGURE 19.5   The search results page contains links to sites that match your search entry.

LOGGING OFF THE INTERNET

When you are finished with your Internet browsing, you need to exit your browser and log off your connection. To exit the browser, click the Close button for the browser. For specific instructions on logging off, check the documentation from your Internet provider. Look for a Sign Out command or Disconnect button.

In this lesson, you learned the basics of Internet browsing. The next lesson covers the basics of Internet e-mail.

Basic E-Mail

In this lesson, you learn how to send and receive e-mail.

Defining E-Mail

E-mail stands for electronic mail, and you can send and receive messages to/from anyone with an e-mail address. There is no real cost associated with sending e-mail. You do pay a price to your Internet service provider for Internet access, but most ISPs do not charge for messages sent and received.

To send and receive e-mail, you need to know what program you have and also your e-mail address.

Which E-Mail Program Do I Have?

To use the e-mail features of the Internet, you need to have a program that can handle e-mail. You may use the program provided by your Internet service provider, or you may use the integrated e-mail programs included with Microsoft's Internet Explorer (Outlook Express Mail) or Netscape Communicator (Netscape Messenger). As another alternative, you may use an online service such as America Online for your mail. Finally, you may purchase and use another e-mail package. For instance, Microsoft Office includes a personal information manager, Outlook, which includes features for handling mail (as well as for scheduling, to-do lists, addresses, and so on).

Most e-mail programs offer comparable features and work in a similar fashion. The exact steps you follow to access mail and send and receive mail will vary from program to program, but you can get the general idea of how mail works by reading this lesson. This lesson uses Outlook Express as the mail program.

You can find out what e-mail program you have by checking the documentation from your Internet service provider. Not only will this tell you how to access mail, but this information will also give you your e-mail address.

What's My E-Mail Address?

To receive mail, you must have an e-mail address, and this address is assigned to you by your Internet service provider. Usually you can select your user name, which often is the first part of your e-mail address. Here's an example of an address:

sohara@iquest.net

The first part is a user name, and the second part defines the server or Internet provider where the mail is sent. The two parts are separated by an at sign (@); an e-mail address always has this sign. Again, check the information sent to you by your ISP to find out your e-mail address.

How Does E-Mail Work?

E-mail works like this. When someone sends you a message, that message is sent to the server that you use for your Internet connection and stored there. When you log on and check your mail, the message is then sent from that server to your PC.

Likewise, when you send mail, you send a message to the recipient's server (where they get the Internet connection). The message is stored there until the recipient checks his or her mail; then the mail is sent to that person's PC.

Starting Your E-Mail Program

To check your mail, you first log on to your Internet service provider and start the mail program. The process will vary depending on which program you use. Usually you start the mail program as you do any other program: with a command or program icon.

ALAP @ BT INT. COM

When you install your e-mail program, that program may put an icon on the desktop. You can double-click this icon to start your mail program. Windows 95, for instance, includes the Inbox icon, which you can use to access Microsoft Exchange.

If you use Netscape Communicator or Internet Explorer, look for a toolbar button or menu command for accessing your mail box.

If you aren't sure, check the information you received from your service provider.

UNDERSTANDING THE E-MAIL PROGRAM WINDOW

Once you start your mail program, you see the program window. Figure 20.1 shows the mail window for Outlook Express. If you use another program, your mail program will look a little differently, but should contain similar features.

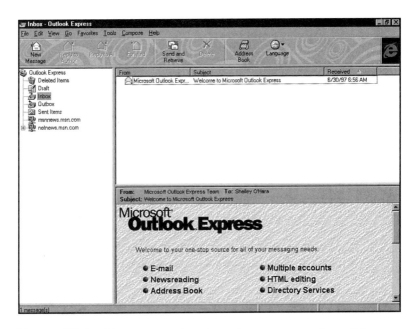

FIGURE 20.1 You can send and receive messages from this e-mail program.

Expect to find a menu bar with commands for accessing all the mail features. Most programs also include a toolbar with buttons you can use as shortcuts to common tasks like checking mail or creating a new message.

Most programs list the message headers in the window. This line tells you the sender, subject, and receive date. You can also usually tell which messages have been read and which have not. For instance, in Outlook Express, bold messages have not been read.

The program window may be divided into panes, like Outlook Express. The left pane lists the folders for handling and storing mail (and also newsgroups). The top right pane contains message headers, and the bottom right pane displays the contents of the selected message.

READING MAIL

Once you get your e-mail address, you can tell your friends, family, and coworkers the address so that they can send you messages. To check your mail, you start the e-mail program, check the mail, and then review any messages in your inbox. Follow these basic steps:

1. Start your e-mail program.

2. Check for new messages. Some programs may check automatically when you start the program. For others, you may have to select a command (or click a shortcut button) to check the mail. You may also have to type a password.

3. Your mail program collects all the messages on your mail server and displays them in your inbox.

4. To read a message, double-click it. You see the contents of the message in a separate message window (see Figure 20.2).

The message window usually includes buttons and commands for handling the message. Your basic options are covered in the next section.

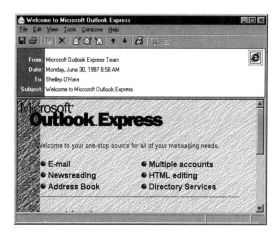

FIGURE 20.2 When you double-click a message header, you see the entire message.

HANDLING MAIL

When you receive a message, you have several choices of what to do with the message:

- **Read and close the message.** To close the message and keep it in your inbox, click the Close (X) button for the message window.

- **Print the message.** To print the message, look for a Print button in the toolbar or a Print command in the File menu.

- **Delete the message.** To delete the message, use the Delete button in the toolbar.

- **Reply to the message.** If you want to send a reply to the sender, click the Reply button in the toolbar. You see a message reply window (see Figure 20.3). When you reply, the address information is complete. The reply may also contain the text of the original message. You can type your response and click the Send button to send the reply.

Figure 20.3   You can reply to messages you have received.

- **Forward the message.** To forward the message to another person, click the Forward button. In the To text box, type the address of that person and then click the Send button.

Depending on the program you have, you may also have other options for handling your e-mail messages.

Sending Mail

You aren't limited to just responding to mail you receive. You can also send an e-mail message to any person with an address. Follow these steps:

1. In your e-mail program, click the New Message button. (The name of this button will vary from program to program.) You can also use a menu command. In Outlook Express, select Compose, New Message. You see a new message window (see Figure 20.4).

2. In the To text box, type the address of the recipient. You can also send a carbon copy and blind carbon copy to other recipients by entering addresses in these fields.

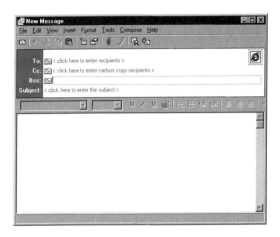

FIGURE 20.4 You can create new messages using this message window.

 Address Book Most mail programs enable you to store frequently used addresses in an address book. You can then look up addresses in this book rather than type them each time. Consult the online help for your mail program for information on using an address book.

3. Type a short description or header for the message in the Subject field.

4. Click in the message area and type your message.

5. To send the message, click the Send button.

You may have other options for sending, depending on the program you are using. For instance, you can assign a priority to the message, attach a file, request a return receipt, and so on.

In this lesson, you learned the basics of Internet e-mail. The next lesson covers some skills for working with Internet newsgroups.

21 LESSON

BASIC NEWSGROUPS

In this lesson, you learn how to work with Internet newsgroups.

DEFINING NEWSGROUPS

If you hear the term newsgroups and think all they deal with is news, you couldn't be more wrong. A newsgroup is an online discussion group, dealing with a wide range of topics.

 Newsgroups The collection of all newsgroups is known as UseNet.

WHAT IS A NEWSGROUP?

What you find in a newsgroup is ordinary people (like you) posting messages. Basically that person can say anything he or she wants in the message, and others can read and respond to the message. The "conversation" isn't live, but is really a series of messages (called a thread). Anyone can open and review the messages at any time. It's like an electronic bulletin board of messages.

Each newsgroup is devoted to a particular topic, and you can find newsgroups on topics ranging from current events to Elvis sightings, from engineering to classical music. There are more than 10,000 newsgroups.

WHAT DOES THE NEWSGROUP NAME MEAN?

There's no way you could read each of the messages in all the newsgroups, so you subscribe to the newsgroups you want. Each newsgroup has a name, and you can usually tell something about the newsgroup from its name. For instance, the following name is pretty self-explanatory:

Rec.outdoors.fishing

The name is divided into categories, and the first part of the name defines the type of newsgroup. Here's a quick list of some of the common newsgroups prefixes:

PREFIX	MEANING
alt	Alternative
comp	Computer
news	General Information about Newsgroups
rec	Recreation
sci	Science
soc	Social
misc	Miscellaneous

You can find many different newsgroups within each category. If there's something of interest to you, there's probably a newsgroup for that topic.

WHAT DO YOU NEED TO PARTICIPATE IN NEWSGROUPS?

To subscribe to and review newsgroup postings, you need a newsreader. You may have received a newsreader program from your Internet service provider. Or you can use the news reader included with Internet Explorer (Outlook Express) or Netscape Communicator (Netscape Collabra).

SUBSCRIBING TO NEWSGROUPS

To read the messages and participate in the newsgroup, you subscribe to the groups you want. The process will vary from one
program to another, but the following are the steps for Outlook
Express:

1. Start your newsreader program. To start Outlook Express,
   click Start, Programs, and Outlook Express.

2. Click the News groups button or open the Tools menu
   and select Newsgroups. (The button you click and command you select will vary if you are using a different program. Look for something similar.)

3. Select the news server you want to use. You may be able
   to choose from several news servers. You should see the
   newsgroups in that server listed.

To See It All If this is the first time you are subscribing,
you may see only a partial list of newsgroups. To view the
complete list, look for an All button or something similar.

---

4. In the newsgroups list, click the newsgroup you want to
   join and click the Subscribe button (see Figure 21.1).

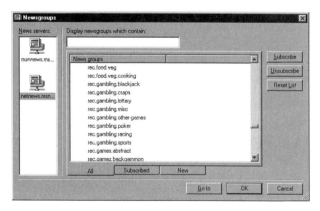

FIGURE 21.1 You can subscribe to any of the listed newsgroups.

5. Continue subscribing to the newsgroups of interest.

6. When you've added all the newsgroups you want, click the OK button.

Reading Newsgroup Messages

Once you have subscribed to a newsgroup, you can review any of the posted messages. Follow these steps:

1. From the news window, select the newsgroup you want to review. In Outlook Express, the newsgroups are listed in the left pane of the window. (You may have to expand the listing to see all of the groups within a certain news server.) To select the newsgroup you want, click it.

   Outlook Express retrieves the messages. Messages that have replies posted to them are marked with a plus sign. You can expand this list to see all of the replies by clicking the plus sign.

2. To read a message, click the name in the list. You see the message (see Figure 21.2).

You can review other messages, select other newsgroups, post replies (covered next), or exit the program. To exit, click the Close button for the newsreader.

When you are reviewing messages, keep in mind that messages are often replies from a previous posting. You may not understand the message you are reviewing because you haven't seen the earlier messages. It's kind of like walking in on the middle of a conversation. If the earlier messages are not posted, you have to kind of guess the gist of the message in some cases.

Also, don't expect to find top-notch quality writing or comments in every postings. You might find that you have to spend some time finding a "good" conversation.

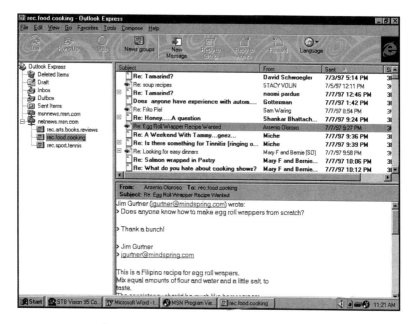

FIGURE 21.2   You can read any of the posted messages in the selected newsgroup.

The messages in these newsgroups are not screened for objectionable content. If you find something offensive, the best thing to do is just unsubscribe from that newsgroup.

Be Careful   It's usually not a good idea to reply to an offensive message and tell that person that you find the message objectionable. If so, you can start a war! Feel free to state your opinion, but remember free speech reigns in these newsgroups. You are better off avoiding groups you find offensive.

Newsgroups often contain a few diehard fans that routinely post and review messages. You may feel as if you are not part of the "clique" when you first get started. Before you start posting messages, read some of the postings to get an idea of the content. Also, look for a FAQ sheet that explains the newsgroup rules.

 FAQ   FAQ stands for Frequently Asked Questions. It is a list of questions and answers you can review to familiarize yourself with the content.

POSTING NEWSGROUP MESSAGES

Reviewing posted messages will give you an idea of the content and participants in a newsgroup. You may want to lurk around, reading messages, to get a feel for the atmosphere. Then when you are ready, you can post your own replies. You can post a reply to an existing message or start a new message. Again, the steps will vary depending on which newsreader you use, but the basic process is similar.

POSTING A REPLY

Follow these steps to post a reply to an existing message using Outlook Express:

1. To reply to an existing message, select that message in the newsreader window.

2. Click the Reply to Group button. (The name of the button will vary. You also can use a menu command.) You see a reply window with the contents of the original posting; the newsgroup is already completed for the To field (see Figure 21.3).

 Replying   You also can reply via e-mail to the sender. To send a message privately, look for a Reply to Author or Reply to Sender button or command.

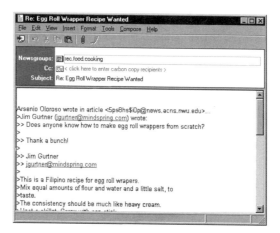

FIGURE 21.3   Complete your reply to the message and click the Post Message button.

3. Click in the message area and type your reply.

4. Click the Post Message button to post the message.

You don't have to reply to an existing message. You can also create a new message, as covered in the next section.

POSTING A NEW MESSAGE

Follow these steps to post a new message to a newsgroup:

1. In the newsreader window, select the group to which you want to post the message.

2. Click the New Message button (or a similarly named button). You can also look for a New Message command. You see a new message window, with the current newsgroup entered in the To field (see Figure 21.4).

3. Type a subject in the Subject line. This line will identify your message in the newsgroup window, so use something descriptive.

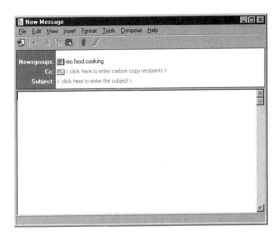

FIGURE 21.4   You can create a new message in a newsgroup by typing the message.

4. Click in the message area and type your message.

5. Click the Post Message button. The message is posted to the newsgroup for others to read and reply to.

In this lesson, you learned the basics of Internet newsgroups. You now know some basic skills for working with the Internet. The next lesson describes using a PC on a network.

USING A PC ON A NETWORK

In this lesson, you learn what a network is.

WHAT IS A NETWORK?

While this book cannot go into a lot of detail about using a PC on a network, you can read this lesson to get an idea of what a network is, why you might use one, and what you can do on a network. You also learn what an intranet is.

A network is a group of interconnected computers, usually linked by some type of cabling system. For instance, all of the PCs in your office might be networked together.

The *server* is the computer that manages the network and contains all the shared information—the files, folders, and programs that anyone connected to the network can access. A *workstation* is one of the individual computers connected to the server. If you have a PC on your desk, that PC is a workstation. You can access the files on the server using your workstation. Keep in mind that people connected to the network cannot access the files on your workstation unless you let them.

WHAT CAN YOU DO ON A NETWORK?

Why set up a network? Your office might have a network so that people in the office can easily share files. Here are some of the things you can do on a network:

- **Send e-mail.** Rather than memos, you can send an e-mail message to a colleague. You have easy access to anyone connected to your network.

- **Share files.** Many projects are collaborations, and it's a hassle shuffling a document using disks. Instead, you can place the files on the server so that those working on the project can access the files.

- **Run programs.** You can run programs placed on the server.

- **Share a printer.** For fast or special printing, your office may invest in a high-speed network printer that everyone can share.

Using a Network

If you have a network, you can check with your system administrator about using the network. For instance, you will need to know how to log on to that network. Logging on is similar to logging on to an Internet service provider. You usually type your user name and password.

You also can find out how to access the files and programs on the network. The system administrator will set up and determine who has access to what files and programs on the PC. If you are hooked up to a network, you can use the Windows 95 Network Neighborhood icon to display and access the files and folders on your network server.

In addition, you should check into how to make your documents available on the network. You may have files you need to share with others in the office.

Finally, you can find out how to take advantage of any other network resources. For instance, have the system administrator set up your printer connection so that you can use the network printer. You might also get your Internet access through your own network. And mail might also be a network option.

WHAT IS AN INTRANET?

In addition to the term network, you may have read or heard
about *intranets*. An intranet is a way to publish information on a
network. Like the Internet, documents can contain text, graphics,
and, most importantly, links to other documents. You navigate
through an intranet just like you do documents on the Internet.

Many companies set up intranets on their networks to publish
company information. For instance, you may be able to review a
company policy handbook online. You might find accounting or
sales information published on the intranet. The ease of navigating through information with links makes an intranet an ideal
way to distribute information.

In this lesson, you learned a little bit about networks and
intranets. You now have a pretty good idea of the most important
computer topics.

INDEX

hard drives, 8
keyboard, 10
memory, 8, 23
microprocessors, 7, 21
monitors, 9-10
motherboards, 7
mouse, 11
power supplies, 8
printers, 12
system box or unit, 7
Compose menu commands
New Message, 134
computers, *see* **PCs**
connecting
Internet, 122-123
keyboard cables, 39
monitor power cords, 39
mouse cables, 39
PC components, 39-41
phone lines, 41
power cords, 39
printers, 39
speakers, 40
troubleshooting, 40
video cables, 39
Control Panel, 60
adding sounds to events, 108
controllers for hard drives, 29
Copy button, 68
copying
files, 89-90
from hard disk to floppies, 90
from one folder to another, 90
with Windows Explorer, 89-90
folders, 85
text, 67-68

cords
monitor power, connecting, 39
power, connecting, 39
Corel Presentations, 19
CPU (central processing unit), 21
creating
folders, 83-84
newsgroups' messages, 142-143
Ctrl (Control) key, 87, 90
customizing Windows 95, 102
Cut button, 67
cutting text, 67-68

D

data files, backing up, 110-111
databases, 18-19
Defragment Now button, 114
defragmenting hard disks, 113-115
Delete button, 133
Delete command, 91
deleting
e-mail messages, 133
files, 90-92
folders, 85
text, 67
desk space, 36
desktop, 43-46
color schemes, 103
displaying memory settings, 23
icons, 44
patterns, 102
shortcuts, 107
Start button, 44-45

Freelance Graphics, 19
freeware programs, 73
Frequently Asked Questions,
see FAQ
FTP sites, 117

G

games, 20
GB (gigabyte), 23
graphics, selecting, 66
graphics programs, 19

H

hand-held scanners, 35
hard disks, 80
    copying files to floppies, 90
    defragmenting, 113-115
    maintaining, 112-115
hard drives, 8, 25, 28-30
    controllers, 29
    viewing drive data, 30
hardware, 1
    joysticks, 35
    maintaining, 115
    modems, 32-34
    requirements for Internet
       access, 118
    scanners, 35
    sound cards, 34
Help, 55-58
    Help Index, 56
    searching for topics, 57
HyperTerminal, 59

I

icons, 44
    Add/Remove Programs,
       74-78
    Inbox, 131
    Internet, 122
    My Computer,
       44, 81, 111-112, 114
    Network Neighborhood, 44
    Recycle Bin, 44, 92
IDE drive controllers, 29
Illustrator program, 19
Inbox icon, 131
increasing memory, 23
inkjet printers, 12
inserting
    CD-ROM discs, 31
    floppy disks, 27
Install button, 75
Install/Uninstall tab, 75, 79
installation programs
    (AutoRun), 75
installing
    DOS programs, 48
    e-mail programs, 131
    programs, 74-77
       with Run command,
       76-77
    Windows 95 components,
       77-78
Intel microprocessors, 22
internal modems, 32
Internet, 116
    activities, 117
       downloading files, 117
       newsgroups, 117
       sending e-mail, 117
       viewing Web pages, 117

connecting, 122-123
disconnecting, 128
logging off, 128
logging on, 122-123
passwords, 122
requirements, 118-121
hardware, 118
ISPs, 118-119
software, 119-121
searching, 126-127
user names, 122
Internet Explorer, 120
Internet icon, 122
Internet service providers,
see ISPs
intranets, 146
ISPs, 118-119, 129-130

J-K

joysticks, 35
KB (kilobytes), 23
Kbps (kilobytes per second), 33
keyboards, 10
cables, connecting, 39
keys
Ctrl (Control), 87, 90
Esc (Escape), 47
Shift, 87

L

laptops, 4
laser printers, 13
lines (phone), connecting, 41
links, 123-125
lists (components), 77
loading e-mail programs,
130-131

logging off Internet, 128
logging on Internet, 122-123
logons (networks), 145
Lotus 1-2-3, 18

M

Macintosh, 4
maintaining
hard disks, 112-115
hardware, 115
programs, 111
manuals, storing, 41
maximizing windows, 54
MB (megabytes), 23
media files, playing, 100
Media folder, 100
Media Player, 59, 99-101
buttons, 100-101
memory, 8, 23
displaying settings, 23
increasing, 23
messages, 133-134
deleting, 133
e-mail, 130
forwarding, 134
newsgroups
creating, 142-143
posting, 141-143
reading, 139-141
replying, 141-142
offensive, 140
printing, 133
reading, 133
replying, 133
reviewing, 139-140
sending, 134-135
MHz (megahertz), 22
microprocessors, 7, 21-22

O

offensive messages, 140
online services (America
Online), 118, 129
Open command (File menu),
97, 100
Open dialog box, 97, 100
opening
documents, 70-71
My Computer, 52
programs, 61-62
windows, 52
operating systems, 14, 42
viewing, 81-83
Windows 95, 3
Windows NT, 3
Outlook Express Mail, 129

P

PageMaker, 17
Paint, 19, 59
Paradox, 19
participating in newsgroups,
137
passwords, 122, 132
networks, 145
Paste button, 68
pasting text, 67-68
patterns for desktop, 102
PCs
components
CD-ROM drives, 8
connecting, 39-41
disk drives, 25
expansion slots, 9
floppy drives, 8

hard drives, 8
keyboard, 10
memory, 8, 23
microprocessors, 7, 21
monitors, 9-10
motherboards, 7
mouse, 11
power supplies, 8
printers, 12
system box or unit, 7
definition, 1
desktop model, 4
laptops, 4
manuals, storing, 41
notebook computers, 4
plugging in, 41
restarting, 46-48
shutting down, 48
tower model, 4
troubleshooting, 42, 47
turning on, 42
types and brands, 3
unpacking, 38-39
Pentium processors, 22
personal information
managers, 20
Phone Dialer, 59
phone jacks, 37
phone lines
connecting, 41
for modems, 33
Photoshop, 19
Play button, 95, 98-100
playing
CDs, 95-96
media files, 100
music, 95-96
sounds, 97-99

troubleshooting
    connecting, 40
    desktop, 46
    PCs, 47
        turning on, 42
    plugging in, 41
turning off PCs, 48
turning on PCs, 41-42
    troubleshooting, 41-42
types
    applications, 14-20
    PCs, 3
    processors, 21
    software, 14

U

undeleting files, 91-92
Uniform Resource Locators,
    see URLs
uninstalling programs, 78-79
unpacking PCs, 38-39
upgrading memory, 23
UPS, 37
URLs, 124
    addresses, 125
UseNet, 136-137
user names, 122
utility programs, 20

V

video cables, connecting, 39
viewing
    disk drives in system, 25
    files, 86-87
        with My Computer, 86
        *with Windows Explorer,
        86-87*

hard drive data, 30
monitors, 38
Web pages, 117
Windows 95's operating
    system, 81-83
Volume Control, 59

W–Z

wallpaper, 102
WAV files, 97-98
Web, 123-124
    browsers, 20
    links, 123-125
    navigating, 124-125
        with addresses, 125
        with links, 124-125
    pages, 123-124
        multimedia, 94
        viewing, 117
    search engines, 126-128
    searching, 126-128
    sites
        Microsoft, 120
        the White House, 124
    surfing, 124-125
        with addresses, 125
        with links, 124-125
windows
    cascading, 55
    closing, 54
    e-mail, 131-132
    maximizing, 54
    minimizing, 54
    moving, 55
    opening, 52
    resizing, 54
    tiling, 55

Complete and Return this Card
for a *FREE* Computer Book Catalog

Thank you for purchasing this book! You have purchased a superior computer book written expressly for your needs. To continue to provide the kind of up-to-date, pertinent coverage you've come to expect from us, we need to hear from you. Please take a minute to complete and return this self-addressed, postage-paid form. In return, we'll send you a free catalog of all our computer books on topics ranging from word processing to programming and the internet.

Mr. ☐   Mrs. ☐   Ms. ☐   Dr. ☐

Name (first) ☐☐☐☐☐☐☐☐☐☐☐ (M.I.) ☐ (last) ☐☐☐☐☐☐☐☐☐☐☐☐☐☐☐

Address ☐☐☐☐☐☐☐☐☐☐☐☐☐☐☐☐☐☐☐☐☐☐☐☐☐☐☐☐
☐☐☐☐☐☐☐☐☐☐☐☐☐☐☐☐☐☐☐☐☐☐☐☐☐☐☐☐

City ☐☐☐☐☐☐☐☐☐☐☐☐☐☐ State ☐☐ Zip ☐☐☐☐☐ ☐☐☐☐

Phone ☐☐☐ ☐☐☐ ☐☐☐☐ Fax ☐☐☐ ☐☐☐ ☐☐☐☐

Company Name ☐☐☐☐☐☐☐☐☐☐☐☐☐☐☐☐☐☐☐☐☐

E-mail address ☐☐☐☐☐☐☐☐☐☐☐☐☐☐☐☐☐☐☐☐☐☐☐☐☐☐

1. Please check at least (3) influencing factors for purchasing this book.

Front or back cover information on book .... ☐
Special approach to the content .... ☐
Completeness of content .... ☐
Author's reputation .... ☐
Publisher's reputation .... ☐
Book cover design or layout .... ☐
Index or table of contents of book .... ☐
Price of book .... ☐
Special effects, graphics, illustrations .... ☐
Other (Please specify): _____ ☐

2. How did you first learn about this book?

Internet Site .... ☐
Saw in Macmillan Computer
    Publishing catalog .... ☐
Recommended by store personnel .... ☐
Saw the book on bookshelf at store .... ☐
Recommended by a friend .... ☐
Received advertisement in the mail .... ☐
Saw an advertisement in: _____ ☐
Read book review in: _____ ☐
Other (Please specify): _____ ☐

3. How many computer books have you purchased in the last six months?

This book only .... ☐   3 to 5 books .... ☐
2 books .... ☐   More than 5 .... ☐

4. Where did you purchase this book?

Bookstore .... ☐
Computer Store .... ☐
Consumer Electronics Store .... ☐
Department Store .... ☐
Office Club .... ☐
Warehouse Club .... ☐
Mail Order .... ☐
Direct from Publisher .... ☐
Internet site .... ☐
Other (Please specify): .... ☐

5. How long have you been using a computer?

Less than 6 months .. ☐   6 months to a year ..... ☐
1 to 3 years .... ☐   More than 3 years ...... ☐

6. What is your level of experience with personal computers and with the subject of this book?

	With PC's	With subject of book
New	☐	☐
Casual	☐	☐
Accomplished	☐	☐
Expert	☐	☐

Source Code — ISBN: 0-7897-1483-3

7. Which of the following best describes your job title?

Administrative Assistant .... ☐
Coordinator .... ☐
Manager/Supervisor .... ☐
Director .... ☐
Vice President .... ☐
President/CEO/COO .... ☐
Lawyer/Doctor/Medical Professional .... ☐
Teacher/Educator/Trainer .... ☐
Engineer/Technician .... ☐
Consultant .... ☐
Not employed/Student/Retired .... ☐
Other (Please specify): .... ☐

8. Which of the following best describes the area of the company your job title falls under?

Accounting .... ☐
Engineering .... ☐
Manufacturing .... ☐
Marketing .... ☐
Operations .... ☐
Sales .... ☐
Other (Please specify): .... ☐

9. What is your age?

Under 20 .... ☐
21-29 .... ☐
30-39 .... ☐
40-49 .... ☐
50-59 .... ☐
60-over .... ☐

10. Are you:

Male .... ☐
Female .... ☐

11. Which computer publications do you read regularly? (Please list)

_____
_____
_____
_____
_____
_____
_____
_____
_____
_____

Comments: _____
_____
_____

Fold here and scotch-tape to mail

‖''|'|''|''|'''''‖|'|'|'|'|''|''|'''‖|'''''‖|'|'|

NO POSTAGE
NECESSARY
IF MAILED
IN THE
UNITED STATES

BUSINESS REPLY MAIL

FIRST-CLASS MAIL PERMIT NO. 9918 INDIANAPOLIS IN

POSTAGE WILL BE PAID BY THE ADDRESSEE

ATTN MARKETING
MACMILLAN COMPUTER PUBLISHING
MACMILLAN PUBLISHING USA
201 W 103RD ST
INDIANAPOLIS IN   46290-9042

MACMILLAN COMPUTER PUBLISHING USA

A VIACOM COMPANY

Technical Support:

If you need assistance with the information in this book or with a CD/Disk accompanying the book, please access the Knowledge Base on our Web site at http://www.superlibrarycom/general/support Our most Frequently Asked Questions are answered there. If you do not find the answer to your questions on our Web site, you may contact Macmillan Technical Support (317) 581-3833 or e-mail us at support@mcpco m.